D1236686

YOUR CHILDREN

WANT to READ

RUTH TOOZE
Director, Children's Book Caravan

YOUR CHILDREN

WANT to READ

A GUIDE FOR TEACHERS AND PARENTS

Englewood Cliffs, N.J.

PRENTICE-HALL, INC.   1957

To
Helen
who helped make Reading
my friend when he was
still a fair-haired boy
and had not yet
become a
problem
child.

Preface

There is great anxiety in our time on the subject of reading. In addition to being an accepted resource for both living and learning it has become a subject to be taught, a problem to wrestle with, a *cause célèbre* with protagonists for this or that approach.

The mass media dominate many lives today—television, radio, movies, comics, and advertising gadgets from signs to awards. Much that is favorable can be said for their content: some of it is very good. But pictures, shortened versions of stories, or condensations of factual material can never really take the place of reading words put together in beauty and truth to inform, to explain, to widen horizons, to deepen understanding, to heighten awareness, to stimulate the mind, and to exalt the spirit. The content of a television show or movie may arouse an interest upon which one can build with reading capable of satisfying the eager learner; in this instance, there is basically no conflict. Reading, however, is and always will be the richest resource for living and learning.

Problems in teaching reading in today's schools arise from many assorted factors: overcrowding of classrooms; having every kind of child with every degree of ability from almost none to that of a genius; changes in our educational philosophy and procedures due to increased knowledge of how a child develops and learns; and occasional over-emphasis on acquiring a skill, with the result that the child fails to become aware of the satisfactions to be experienced from its use. Here, then, is a book dealing informally with many aspects of this whole concern over reading: what reading really is; about children and how they learn; about the social order and education procedures today; about some of the many books which can and should be a rich resource for both the living and learning of American children; and about some fine authors whom our children are fortunate in having as friends. Neither a study of children's literature nor a textbook for the teaching of reading, *Your Children Want to Read* nevertheless opens a few important doors for its readers. It has been written for teachers and parents, and it is intended to stimulate their thinking and careful analysis of reading in our kind of social order and to provide some specific knowledge of books and authors to meet the needs and interests of today's growing child.

RUTH TOOZE

Contents

1

What Is Reading?

Panel discussion of reading · Several definitions of reading · Problems arising from the skill approach · Today's slow readers and non-readers · Need for teachers to know many books · Need for easily available books · Reading as a part of living and learning today

4

Changing Concepts in Meeting Children's Needs and Interests

The six- to eight-year-old child in the primary grades · Physical characteristics · Psychological characteristics · Vocabulary and readiness to read · Type face and general appearance of a printed page · Some books printed in various readable type faces · Interesting content · Humor · Comics growing from room activities · Picture dictionaries · Other educational reading devices

The nine- to eleven-year-old child in grades 4, 5, and 6 · Physical changes · Group interest · Increase in vocabulary and breadth of interests · Other people and hero-worship · Active reading period

The twelve- to fourteen-year-old child in grades 7, 8, and 9 · Adolescent physical and behavioral changes and increased interest in ideas · Appealing book format · Changing patterns · Conflicting interests

Summary of desirable goals and probable achievements

5

Books to Help Children Understand and Adjust to the Physical World

For children up to the age of eight · Beginnings of life · Growth · Life cycles of animals · Plants and trees · Earth and sky · General science · True-to-life stories

8

Reading in Terms of Life 213

YOUR CHILDREN

WANT to READ

1

What Is Reading?

"Wish I had never agreed to be on this panel on reading!" exploded Marian to Janet as they walked up the steps to the afternoon session of the annual conference.

"I'm glad I'm just the recorder, so at least I don't have to say anything," said Janet.

"You were wise, but Miss Hurlbut made me feel it was an honor to be asked, so I couldn't refuse. But, honestly, the more I think about it the more confused I am. Teaching reading isn't anything like it was when I began teaching twelve years ago.

3

Then you followed the manual, most children took the readers as they came, and all but two or three got along all right. Now, half of them 'hate' reading, meaning that they can't read and won't try to learn. Of course, nobody wants to do what he can't do with some satisfaction to himself. And it isn't all due to television."

"Of course it isn't. My children say the readers are 'dumb' and 'uninteresting.' You cannot make a child today do something merely because you say so. He has to be interested. I sometimes wonder if our readers are good enough to hold children's interest."

"That's what I'm supposed to talk about—adequate motivation. I know that just learning the new words in each reader isn't adequate for most of my children. The new pictures help, but actually they are so obvious and the 'sissy' type. One of my boys said yesterday, 'Nothing ever happens.' These readers don't have much appeal for children who look at television hours each day and go to movies once or twice a week. But do I dare say that?"

"I think you'll have to be honest, Marian. You're a good third grade teacher with twelve years' experience. You *should* know something about teaching reading; it's what you are chiefly paid to do."

"I know, Janet, but each year I seem less sure about how to teach it. Sometimes I wonder if reading is as important in today's living as we used to think it was. I haven't cracked a book this year, have you?"

"Yes, several. I must read to be happy. Look, there's that redhead, the new teacher at Washington. He is just out of the Air Force."

At the door of the meeting room, a crowd was pouring in. The reading section was drawing the largest number of people. All around them, the air was full of eager interest and many questions.

The moderator introduced the five panel members, and said,

"This afternoon we are going to discuss what reading is and whether it should occupy the important place in the classroom today that it has for so long. Everyone says that it is still our chief means of learning, that success in arithmetic, history, and literature depends upon whether the child can read. If this is true and reading is that important, why are we having so many difficulties today—so many slow readers, so many non-readers, and so much criticism by parents and educators of the way we teach reading?

"Mr. Bowles, you are a parent and teacher of long experience in the seventh grade. Will you start our thinking together?"

Mr. Bowles, a man with a sensitive face and kindly eyes, said, "May I ask a question? Are we talking about school reading or outside reading?"

Mr. Hunter, the young sixth grade teacher just back from two years in the army, could hardly wait for the chair's recognition.

"Outside reading! Outside what? The classroom? Life? That's it," he continued, "there can't be all these different kinds: *school* reading, *outside* reading, *work-type* reading, *supplementary* reading, *classroom* reading, *Friday* reading. This last description 'got me' during my first week back at school. On Friday, one of the boys said, 'Gee, Friday at last, so we can have Friday reading!'

" 'What did you say?' I asked.

" 'Friday reading. You know, good books, real stuff, not just the dumb ol' textbooks. Fridays we can read real books, so we call it Friday reading.'

"I was floored. What has happened to us? To think that the worlds which books open to people get categorized as 'Friday reading' because we set such limits! Reading opens the doors to the universe today and always will. Oh, sure, there are television and radio and movies and picture magazines. But the bulk of information, knowledge, and inspiration to clear thinking is in books to be read Monday, Tuesday, Wednesday, Thursday, Friday—any day, every day. Reading is reading—guess I'd say as

Gertrude Stein might, 'Reading is reading is reading is reading.'"

He remembered that this was a panel and that no one should make a speech, so he stopped. "Must be a highbrow," whispered one teacher to her neighbor.

All the members of the panel, even Marian, were on the edge of their chairs, as was half the audience.

"I agree with Mr. Hunter," said Miss Webb, a popular fifth grade teacher. "Reading is part of the all-round development of people, both children and adults. A book may contain the whole of life. It really is the highest form of shared experience. Through it one can share the best thinking any really great person has ever done. Surely we want to keep this door wide open for our children."

The redhead, Mr. Lowrey, asking for the chair's recognition, was soon granted it. He unfolded his long legs and stood up.

"Mr. Chairman and fellow teachers. I'm new here, new at teaching seventh graders, too, but my kids and I seem to have a lot in common. I'm just back from four years in the Air Force. We had to teach a large number of men, who couldn't read much, a great deal, and do it quickly. We had film strips and many movies, even comics written to order about our work. They learned the words and the subjects fast. What we need in school today is more audio-visual resources—projectors, good movies, film strips, maybe television in every room—if we are going to teach these kids successfully. Those are today's techniques. Oh, you have to know some basic words to get along, but these new techniques really put the subject across."

Mr. Hunter came back quickly, "Reading means more than just the skill needed to acquire information. Reading is more than the sum of the word meanings on a printed page. Ever listen to music, Mr. Lowrey?"

"Yes, but you don't have to think to listen to music," answered Mr. Lowrey.

"You don't?" asked Mr. Hunter. "What about a symphony?

The more you know about its form and pattern, the more you enjoy it."

"That's outside my experience," said Mr. Lowrey.

"It is obvious that we represent a wide range of experience here, a wide range of attitudes toward this very fundamental problem in our teaching," said the moderator. "I realize that many of you consider reading fundamental to the whole business of living long after we have left the classroom." He wondered how he could keep the discussion amicable and give adequate recognition to each point of view.

No recorder ever had quite so strenuous a job as Janet's for the next two hours.

"Don't miss that, Miss Gill," the moderator would say, or, "Did you get his exact words on that?"

Finally the session had to close.

"This is the best discussion I have ever shared with a group of teachers," said the moderator. "I came here with a set of questions to put before the group, but there was not even time to present them.

"Just what is reading?

"Will it survive in our kind of civilization?

"Is the increasing development of many audio-visual resources going to limit its functions?

"If it is to survive, who will read and how?

"What makes people—both children and adults—want to read?

"We have tried to answer these questions and many more, and at least started our thinking on many aspects of this concern of ours. As I sat here, I was reminded of a recent afternoon with Carl Sandburg, who was to talk on poetry. Mr. Sandburg said that when he prepared his lecture, he thought he would start by defining poetry. After several hours, he found that he had 267 definitions, 'each one better than the last, no matter where you begin,' he told us. He read 67 of those definitions and suggested that each of us might like to go on and make our own additional 200.

"Actually we have given many definitions of reading this afternoon and discussed many aspects of its value and function in living and learning in our world today. Much of this will start whole new trains of thought for each of us as we return to our classrooms. Perhaps some of you may want to set up some study groups to continue our thinking. How many would like a summary of this discussion, perhaps best done by listing these various definitions or concepts, with a few of the most apt comments on them?"

The affirmative response was unanimous.

As the group broke up, one could hear continuing discussion and various comments on all sides.

"This is it."

"Good, wasn't it?"

"Yes, more honest than we usually are."

"Makes me think."

Mr. Hunter turned around and said, "Yes, if we can really think of what each child needs rather than merely follow a standardized process of teaching each grade, maybe we won't feel so stymied over teaching. I got out of the army fired with a desire to help prepare kids for the world as it is today. I felt my own education did not do that. But I was going to resign at the end of this year because I thought I could not buck established methods. Maybe I'll stick another year and see whether I can get more books and other resources, and release my kids to learn. They have plenty of curiosity and enthusiasm. If only we did not kill it! We go on teaching the same way we did twenty-five years ago, while all the growth in biology, physiology, anthropology shows us that we only learn what we live. We have to give them a chance to live in the classroom. Here I am on my soapbox again. I'll get down, but boy, these kids get me!"

Here are some of the definitions Janet took down that afternoon, with some of the comments made on them:

1. Reading is a rich resource for living and learning.

2. Reading gives accurate and necessary information about the world around us, about people in other places, about people and events of the past.

3. Reading offers stimulation to thought through discovery of what great thinkers of the past have thought, through ideas related to and evolving from current living.

4. Reading offers inspiration for spiritual awareness and spiritual growth.

5. Reading is an interesting experience, often a highly pleasurable one, often real fun.

6. Reading, writing, speaking, and listening are aspects of language arts. Of these four, reading is perhaps the most important.

7. Reading is far more than a skill, although it involves several skills.

8. Reading is one of the forms of communication. It is communication without the limitations of time and space. A reader may go where he will, when he will, in reality or in imagination.

9. Reading is a form of behavior, and must not only be understood as such, but also thought of in relation to other forms of behavior.

10. Reading is part of the all-round development of both children and adults. The more fully a child lives, the more easily he learns to read, and the more reading becomes a part of his everyday living. In the beginning, the child actually learns to read when he is ready, because of a certain combination of circumstances and his own growth, much as he walks and talks when he is ready. Gradually, as he sees the need for reading to achieve certain desired goals and to carry out certain purposes and observes it used by others for such objectives, he is likely to want to use it himself to fulfill those needs.

11. Reading is closely related to general growth and contributes to it, equipping the child in many ways for easier and more wholesome maturation. It is essential to success in any

work, an important realization for a child to acquire early. Awareness of its part in an adult's success may offer a dynamic motivation for reading. As the child grows through reading activities, he also grows in his reading abilities.

12. Reading illumines experience. For a young child, it is an extension of his early language abilities. Some psychologists say that reading is a child's first observation, as he looks at any given object and attempts to discover its meaning for himself. When we extend this process, reading becomes naturally and easily a handle into the reality of living.

13. Reading contributes to the individual's sense of relationship to the universe, thus aiding in his adjustment to himself and to others, and to the physical, intellectual, and spiritual worlds.

14. Reading offers opportunity for identification with another who has like problems, like characteristics. Thus, through reading a biography of someone with a similar personality or a story in which the hero or heroine is like oneself, emotional adjustment is often aided or more easily made.

15. Reading is accepted by all people who live fully.

16. Reading is an easy way to satisfy many needs.

17. Reading is one of the "keys to the kingdom"—the kingdom of earth, the kingdom of heaven.

Study groups in conferences or as part of in-service training like the one above and discussions in current magazines, books, and at public meetings all show that American education needs to do some real thinking about the place of the three "R's" and the way they are being taught, especially the reading "R."

Obviously, reading is a valuable key for every good citizen to possess and use. Our modern philosophy of education, accepting most of what has been suggested about the place of reading as important in today's living, sees reading as a means, not an end in itself. But the practice in schools is often far from this philosophy. Reading is still a skill to be learned in many places. In a skill approach to reading, mastery of the skill often becomes an end in itself. Frequently, also, reading becomes just busy work.

The content of much material offered to the beginning reader is often much too limited for the dimensions of many children's needs and interests. Many children are bored and develop a wrong attitude toward what reading is, misconceiving not only what it can be, but what it should be. To demand any skill before a child has use for it may evoke antagonism instead of interest and cooperation. This early antagonism may give rise to emotional problems which make the child hate reading because it seems to have no meaning for him—no value in his business of living, no answering of his needs, no direct relationship to his world.

Dick was not quite five when his grandmother came to visit the new home near the camp where his father had been recalled to active service in the marines. Fortunately, his mother had found a kindergarten in which he was happy. He was eager to show his school to his grandmother, so they went in her car, soon after her arrival, to see it. As they pulled up beside the curb of the house where it was held, two "big" six-year-old boys were playing in the yard. Dick became quite excited and exclaimed, "There are the Oh Oh boys."

"What are the *Oh Oh boys*, Dick?" his grandmother asked.

"Why, they are the boys who have their own books to read. They read: 'Run, Jimmie, run. Oh, Oh.

     "Run, run, run. Oh, Oh.

     "Look, look, look. Oh, Oh.'

"Grandmother, when you and I read, it is so much fun. When I get to be as big as a real Oh Oh boy, is it going to be that dumb?"

Experiences like this in the first grade here, there, and everywhere are far too common these days for us to ignore them with a laugh. The content of what we offer children for their initial reading experience merits careful consideration.

Obviously, there is no "great literature" for the six-year-old. Just what are his reading needs? The necessity for clear, honest thinking about this question is evident. To try to develop a skill arbitrarily as a basis for meeting future vital requirements is not in line with today's philosophy of teaching. What, then, are children to read in the beginning, and for what purposes? Can reading be meaningful to children of six and seven years? We believe that it can, and that the process need not obstruct actual experience of true value to each growing individual.

In a skill approach, too often the mastery of the skill becomes not only an end in itself, but also establishes the standard or measure of success in school. This not only gives the child a false set of values, but bewilders him. Readers are not robots; they are created individually, not produced by any mass production. We shall consider individual basic needs and ways of meeting these more fully in later chapters.

Frequently, too great emphasis is put upon words themselves. Often, a textbook gives just one interpretation—just one point of view—which the reader tends to consider an absolute truth rather than just one form of presentation. Word emphasis may also create unfortunate stereotypes. A child who knows how to read, but does not really read more than successive individual words, may develop inadequate and unfair concepts of history, people, relationships, and values.

The skill approach does not always give adequate value and recognition to the various ways of learning. To recognize certain words is no sure path to learning. It helps, but it needs blending with many forms of activities and understandings. In any group situation, different ways of learning should be evaluated and appreciated.

The skill approach too often puts a premium on this one form of success rather than on the well-rounded development of the child. Sometimes, all that is being taught is failure. To many children, the resultant loss in self-respect becomes a handicap for life.

Joe, fourteen and in sixth grade, was an uncooperative non-reader, marking time until he became sixteen and could leave school. While his room was listening to a storyteller and looking at a special book exhibit, he was noisy and disturbing. Later, he came up to the storyteller and said, "Hi! My name's Joe Tagliaferro. Know how to spell it?"

She answered quickly, "Think I do. T-a-g-l-i-a-f-e-r-r-o."

"Gosh," he said. "You really do. How'd you know? Ain't it awful to have a name like that? If you can pronounce it, you can't spell it. If you can spell it, you can't pronounce it."

"Yes," she said, "I know. I have a rather bad one myself. There was a famous actress by that name, Maggie Tagliaferro."

"There was? Ever see her?"

"Yes, I did."

"And was she good?"

"One of the best."

"Have you got any books about Wops?" he asked suddenly.

There weren't many: *The Roman Moon Mystery,* a book for junior high school age and a biography of Marconi, also for older children. And this boy couldn't read well.

But she tried him out. "Like mysteries?"

"Sure. Listen to 'em every night."

"How would you like to read one—this is good!"

He picked it up. "Those Wops lived a long time ago."

She continued, "Yes, but people don't change very much."

He came right back, "Mussolini was sure a skunk."

But he went off with the two books.

He came back the next afternoon. "I'm sure glad you came to our school. I read those books. They're good."

"Why did you want books about Wops?" she asked.

"Well, I'll tell you," he said. "My mother always thought we were French. Then she found out we were just Wops. Boy, did that ever burn her up! Want to know something? I'm going home this afternoon for the first time in my life with something to make my mother happy. I can tell her, 'It ain't so bad to be a Wop,' 'cause I know. I found that out in those books. It's funny how much there is in a book. I never read 'em much. Always thought they were dumb—but I think I'll look for some more now. As I said, Ma'am, it's kind of lucky for me you came to our school."

A lecturer on books who talks to junior high and high school students is disturbed at the ever-recurring inquiry, "Aren't there any *thin* books for which one can get credit?" Reading is evidently not a meaningful experience in their lives. Besides, there isn't enough time for it.

Comments like these are common when a group of high school English teachers meet to discuss their problems. "What do you do with the children who cannot read the books on your required list?"

"More than half of my sophomores just cannot read *Ivanhoe* or *Julius Caesar*."

"Why don't they teach children to read in the elementary school?"

"My children dislike reading so much they resent me as an English teacher."

"All children hate English."

"Actually, English in high school has meaning for only about a fourth of the children."

These are direct quotations from conference groups in different parts of the United States. One could multiply them indefinitely.

One of the large publishers of textbooks found sales declining in recent years. Competition with other text series could not account for such a universal decline, so they started a survey. Reports from many areas said their material was too difficult to be read by the grade for which it was intended. They continued the survey, including the reading series of other publishers now used in most public schools. Reports tallied generally as follows (grades four through eight):

	Per cent
Can read the book, be stimulated to go on to other reading	10 to 15
Can read and understand the content	20 to 25
Can read the words and understand some of the content	20 to 25
Cannot read the book at all	45 to 55

So, this one publisher is having its series rewritten using a vocabulary down at the level of the 45 to 55 per cent. Surely this is not the answer. But the fact that it can happen at least partially supports the critics who say that today's schools are being increasingly geared down to the level of the least able children. This is far too general a situation to ignore or treat lightly.

Another group of people are rewriting our classics in simple language for the so-called non-reader or slow reader. Why do we read classics? For the plot line or for the beauty of words put together to communicate experience, joy, sorrow, living to the reader?

Another group think that all stories and all informative material should be presented to children in three or four forms, from an easy level to a standard level for a given age or grade. Thus, the third grade would have a given curriculum, with all materials related to each subject area in science, mathematics, and social studies presented in three or four different ways for different levels of reading ability. So, also, would the fourth and fifth and sixth grades. What assurance has any teacher that Johnny, who reads at level one in grade three, has to stay there in all succeeding grades?

Schools hire more and more remedial reading teachers; reports say they are one of the highest salaried groups today. All this indicates that reading is more often a problem than an enriching resource for living in the modern school. Why? How does it come about that the slow reader and the non-reader have become so great a concern in our schools? There is no sim-

ple answer, for many factors enter this situation. We may find
some help as we explore further.

A far larger number of children of all levels of ability are in
school today than formerly. Reading involves many skills, most
of which grow through use, and in reading, as in all areas of
learning, they learn what they live. But no one will read who
does not derive joy and satisfaction from the doing. Of what
use is this wonderful key if few care to use it, either because
they do not know or care about the riches in the rooms it opens,
or because the process of using it is too difficult. Since the natural abilities of the enlarged school population extend over so
wide a range, no single approach can satisfy the wide extent of
their needs.

Perhaps, too, this emphasis upon the process, the skill in and
of itself, may be one cause of the prevalent reading problems
and antipathies. Most schools use a basal series of readers to
"teach reading." Each of these basal series has a system of readiness—preparation, analysis, and word-recognition guaranteed
to give sure-fire results to the users. All the series have many
factors in common although differing in some details, but the
producers of each series are certain of the results attainable by
its faithful usage. One sometimes wonders whether, after all
the preparatory steps to get ready to prepare to begin to com-
mence to start to read, both teacher and child are not too ex-
hausted to actually read.

This is not to say that much of this material is not good. It is.
But its appeal is to middle-class American children, with far too
little content which can appeal to the large number of children
in academic and upper class groups or children at the other end
in industrial, mining and many other lower income groups.
Hence, it is related to the lives of some children, but not all.
Much of the content is not sufficiently interesting to lure a child
on to further use of this wonderful skill, this key to fuller living.

Under existing procedures, individual learning at one's own
rate of speed is frequently not possible, despite all the work-

shops, courses, and books about reading that tell us this is the *only* way children *really* learn to read. The increasing number of diagnostic clinics, general reading clinics, workshops, and in-service training courses are indications of the great awareness of this problem. Most teachers are ready and eager to find better ways to develop reading in our learning and living situations today.

If we are honest, we must admit the increase in the number of slow readers and non-readers in school today. There are many children who do not like to read, who still do everything else imaginable before opening a book. We use the general term *slow readers* for this group, but they are not all alike.

The reasons for their lack of interest in reading are nearly as varied and numerous as the children themselves. Handicaps of sight and hearing account for a few; discovery of such handicaps should be made early and adequate help given as soon as possible.

There are a small number of *mirror readers* who see things in reverse. These are easily identifiable, and there are methods for correcting this defect.

Another group are *pure act* children, so active they find it difficult to ever settle down to do anything which does not involve much action.

A few have an unusually short eye span, and to them the average length of a line of type in most books presents an almost insurmountable difficulty.

There are also emotional blocks of many kinds which prevent many children from reading or even trying hard enough to acquire a liking for it. For instance, the child whose mother reads so much he feels it prevents her giving him sufficient attention may develop a serious block against it because he resents the competition of reading with his needs. Or, too much may have been demanded of a child too early, with punishment for failure.

Some parents blame the way reading is taught in schools today for their children's lack of ability to read easily, believing that the so-called word method is not good or that more phonics or more drill is needed.

The competition for a child's time and interest by radio, television, comics, and movies tends to develop a strong awareness of the most exciting or funniest current interest. We live in a swiftly paced era, when we want what we want in a hurry, and haven't time to read what we might get (or think we might) from pictures.

We live in a time of over-stimulation which tends to make many children willing to give time only to what is exciting, making them impatient with anything that moves slowly or is not in the "thriller" class.

We live in a time when the newspaper, the magazine, the tabloid, the picture magazine, the comics, the picture advertisement all present news, information, and ideas to us in vivid, telling pictures, so that picture-reading (not just looking at pictures) is far more a part of the learning pattern than it used to be. We live in a time when a wide variety of audio-visual resources help us to learn and be entertained in realms formerly accessible to us only through reading.

Children are great imitators. Much of their learning takes place through imitation. Many of them come from homes where they see little reading take place, where the daily paper and a few magazines are about all Mom and Pop have time for, where there are few books, if any at all.

So we are increasingly aware of reluctant readers in schools everywhere—in cities, towns, villages, and rural areas. There is much that can be done to help these children by recognizing the problem and its many causes, by acknowledging the children's needs, and by knowing and making easily available the right kinds of books in various situations.

Even admitting that this group may be 40 to 50 per cent of the average class, what of the other 50 to 60 per cent? Surely all of these children ought to have their needs and interests met as fully as possible, and this, undoubtedly, involves many problems in addition to concern over skill in reading. Much material should be easily available. The teacher needs to know books of all kinds, their content, the way they can meet both curricular interests and the specific needs of individual children. A non-reading teacher is apt to have fewer good readers in his room.

There can well be much more pupil-teacher planning and discussion of both materials and ways of using them; more encouragement for different ways of learning with reading many kinds of material related to the subject being studied, in story books, biographies, encyclopedias, dictionaries, magazines, newspapers; in reports by groups and individuals; in map drawing, murals, dramatization. All these involve reading for many purposes.

Reading becomes an inherent part of learning situations which are living situations in which each child finds a way to use all his abilities, receives recognition for his contribution to the group, and gains a sense of adequacy in doing what facilitates his own happiness and usefulness.

This book does not offer any new method for teaching reading. It tries to indicate some of the factors involved in the status of reading in a democratic social order, to consider some of the basic needs of children today and conditioning factors in our schools and homes, and to discuss some of the materials most likely to be of interest in meeting personal, social, and curricular needs and interests. It is written with the sincere belief that reading is going to be an important resource for living and learning for a long time to come, and with the realization that there is today great need for a warmer human approach to the whole subject.

2

Why Read?

*W*E live in a democracy. A part of the democratic concept is that it makes possible opportunities for individuals to develop to the measure of which they are capable of assuming responsibility. Literacy is considered essential for such development, not literacy for just a favored few, but literacy for everyone. This point of view assumes that all men can read, and that, if given a chance, all men want to read.

If this is an assumption of the democratic way of life, then it is an essential responsibility of the school and home in our social order to develop living learning–situations in which all the means, including reading, for growing into happy, useful citizens are utilized.

In a democracy, each citizen has certain needs. There is a great need for accurate information in order that a citizen may base his judgments upon true knowledge of all factors involved, whether he is voting, serving on a committee, or holding an office. Wise choices and wise decisions need accurate information first. A scientist, a teacher, a doctor, a lawyer, a surveyor, all need accurate information first. Most of such information at the present time is available only through books.

There is great need for clearer understanding: understanding of people, how they think, react, work; understanding of how people have acted in the past, the results of which created our present situation; understanding of conflicting motives at work in the community, state, nation, world; understanding of ideas which work for the good of the whole.

Every citizen should be objective in his judgments. He must be able to weigh the ideas of others, evaluate them, sift propaganda from informative data; then he will be able to make sound judgments as they are needed. Both the individual and the groups through which he serves will make wiser choices contributing to the good of all the citizenry if such objectivity is developed.

From the many demands for his time and thought and service, the good citizen makes discriminating selection of that to which he gives his attention. Because reading may help a citizen satisfy his needs for background, accurate facts and information, the stimulus of knowing how others have worked on similar problems, the inspiration of the best thinking of mankind, it is an essential resource for his better functioning in the democratic process.

The problem of making it easy and possible for all children to read is not as simple as just indicating its importance may sound. Despite much good planning, there are many difficulties in working out mass education in America. Many class-

rooms are overcrowded. It is much more difficult to help individuals grow and learn at their own rate of speed and in their
own ways with 40 to 50 pupils in the classroom than it is with
25. Overcrowding creates many difficulties.

Teachers feel frustrated. The increasingly large number of
children flooding today's schools means that schools have many
teachers who are not well-trained. If a well-trained teacher is
overwhelmed and frustrated by her classroom situation, how
much more so is one who is inadequately trained!

The rapid rate of increase which far exceeds the community's
planning in school space and materials means not only overcrowding, but also forces both teacher and children to work
with insufficient materials. This situation may stimulate some
creativity: some needs can be met by making things. Books,
however, are not one of such needs. Children may make shelves
or movable carriers for their books, but the books themselves
need to be provided in such quantities as to meet thousands of
needs of all types at all levels of reading ability.

Certain characteristics of this twentieth century are important to consider in attempting to find the true place of reading
in our pattern of living. There are great changes, not only in
how we live and grow, but also in what we know about how
to live and grow best, due to the great scientific discoveries of
our times. How does this increase of scientific knowledge, this
increase of scientific ways of doing things, affect home and
school living? It creates a very different environment from that
of a generation ago. Knowledge of the atom bomb brings a
whole new set of fears into a child's consciousness. Labor-saving
devices mean less work for all members of the family in main-
taining a home—less opportunity for children to share work and
responsibility and increased leisure time. Many scientific discoveries prolong life, but society has not found what to do with
so many older people. Better care is taken of the mentally disturbed, but institutions have more patients each year. Psychi-
atry shows us the results of emotional disturbances in the lives

of young children, but we are not able to do much about the broken homes caused by war and other social disorders which create more and more such disturbances. Some children live in environments where only instruments of destruction are made. Heavy taxes, most of which go for military purposes, mean less money for wholesome family uses. These are but a few of the many changes due to rapid scientific development. The results of all of this scientific change do not always work for the welfare of mankind; the problems they create challenge everyone concerned with children's well-being.

The tremendous increase in the field of knowledge makes a great difference in what the individual can and should learn. It is no longer humanly possible to know even a little about all that mankind has learned and is learning. An individual cannot relive the entire experience of mankind. Thus, choices must be made, constantly and consistently.

Training in how to make choices has become a primary responsibility of education today. Much study consists of summaries of high peaks in given areas of knowledge. Intensive study can take place only in one small area, so specialization is a need of the day. This specializing is good in some ways, especially in the development of detailed knowledge in a given area; but it is harmful in other ways in that it frequently causes a lack of balance in developing procedures because of insufficient knowledge of qualifying factors in related areas. For children, it means confusion, bewilderment, and too many pressures. The child's problem of finding his place, the special contribution he can make in so vast and complicated a world, is a serious one today. The teacher's skill in helping him gain enough general background and adequate special knowledge for his own best functioning often means mental and physical health or mental and physical illness for the child. In this situation a tremendous responsibility rests upon the teacher of today. He should, of course, possess knowledge; but, through reading, he must continually develop vision and wisdom for guidance of children.

This aspect of education concerns not only the guidance counsellor in high school, but every teacher from the first grade up.

The increase in both speed and means of communication means that our world has changed from an assortment of isolated, independent nations or communities, knowing and caring little about each other, to an interdependent brotherhood. The very existence of this new world depends upon nations knowing themselves and each other and respecting the common needs so that each may live adequately according to his own needs and desires. This interdependence is not only economic, but political, ideological, and spiritual.

Tommy, who lives on a farm in the middle of the United States, no longer can be content to learn merely about corn and wheat-growing, soil characteristics of his region, and marketing procedures in nearby cities in order to run successfully the farm he inherits. Now he must know the farm needs of this nation and of other nations; he must be aware of the thousand factors that condition the farmer's life today. If Pakistan grows enough wheat for her own nation and India, will religious differences between these two nations permit adequate sharing? Does the present development of communist ideology since Stalin's death mean more gifts of wheat by Russia to needy areas of the world, thus taking away past customers of the United States and thereby threatening our crop values?

International relations affect every child's life today. The speed of interchange of information about any activity in the world permits no one to live in isolation. What is happening in Indonesia or Yugoslavia today affects the pattern of every American child's life. Much of such necessary information must be acquired by reading the newspapers, journals of opinion, and books of both information and interpretation. The uninformed person is inadequately equipped for living today.

The increase in both speed and methods of transportation, added to the development of communication, means a far greater mobility of both man and goods than has ever existed in the history of mankind. Almost every corner of the globe is today easily accessible by automobile, train, ship, or airplane. Anyone may know everyone. People on the other side of the world are neighbors, no longer strangers or heathen. Produce and products may be easily shipped to any place they are needed, so that a country with a limited area but great manufacturing capacities can import raw materials, while an agricultural nation can import manufactured products. This interdependence steadily increases. Self-sufficiency becomes less and less feasible. Thus, the need to know more and more about other lands, other economies, other patterns of living and other people, grows and grows.

The social studies no longer consist only of some knowledge of physical characteristics of each continent and a superficial acquaintance with the history of many peoples; they have become a vital necessity to every child for understanding himself and how he came to be as he is. They have become an essential means not only for understanding other people, but also for seeing how human beings of so many kinds may live together on one good earth. Differences should become bases for friendly understanding rather than hostility. A personal human force lies back of all history and geography study today, giving it motivation such as has never existed before. This motivation is deep-seated in all learning situations. Even superficially, the child's experience with all means of transportation, e.g., the increasing interest in planes and flying, means a new approach to the social studies as well as to science and mathematics. Air age mapping is very different from other mapping. A vast proportion of the information needed for such learning and living can be gained through reading.

The greater speed of communication, transportation, and every kind of exchange of both goods and ideas means an overwhelming increase in the whole tempo of living. It is so difficult to do so much that one must hurry, hurry, hurry to get it all done. This is why tabloids, news summaries, and magazines

which give the gist of articles in other magazines are furnished;
thus, he who runs may read and keep abreast of the times. All
too frequently, this makes for superficiality. The thorough
worker, the careful craftsman, the perfectionist do not fit into
today's pattern of living. There isn't time. A premium is put
upon speed. Teachers will do well to try to discover the importance of the element of speed in most tests that we admin-
ister today, and to try to evaluate honestly its relative significance.

This increased tempo of living means that many children
constantly feel pressed for time in which to crowd all the activities possible, and thus they are constantly over-stimulated. This
fact is undoubtedly responsible for many of the tensions of today—tensions which seldom contribute to good health or healthful living.

Some human beings are slow-paced. Is there any place for
them in this rushing scheme of today's living? What is time for?
Over and over one hears as an excuse for not doing something
in the classroom or at home, "There just isn't time." There is for
everyone—*all the time there is.* Again, it is important to help
children make choices so that they have time for all the activities essential to their needs—including reading, which often
takes time.

The rapid growth of all the mass media of communication
has altered our whole pattern of living and profoundly influenced values in today's social order. Television, radio, movies,
and comics probably exert the most powerful determining
influence in children's lives today. They have hold of our children's growing edges.

A recent experience of a visiting lecturer in one of the Philadelphia schools is revealing. She was discussing interesting
books with the seventh and eighth graders and the talk turned
toward biographies of interesting people.

One boy said, "You know, by the time you have been in school as *long* as we have, you get sick and tired of reading about so many people that are dead!"

She suggested that when those people were alive, they were exciting, dynamic people—full of original ideas—who often changed the whole pattern of life because of what they thought and did. Then she said, "You can only understand yourselves as you know those people, for you are what you are because of what they were and the things they did."

"Do you mean that? I wish any history teacher I ever had ever thought that. I never heard anyone say that what those old guys did had anything to do with me."

Then she said to the group, "Fifty years from now, one hundred years from now, a group of children like you will be sitting here in this classroom or one near here, trying to understand what the middle of the twentieth century was really like. To do this, they will probably read the lives of certain outstanding people, people who influenced our life, people who are characteristic of our time. Who will be the people they will be reading about?"

There was a long silence. Finally, the most studious boy in the group, an eighth grader said, "First of all, Hop-a-long Cassidy."

No one laughed. They talked it over a while, and at last all agreed *he* would be the most important one to know.

Their second choice was Einstein.

The next choices were men from the sports world, military world, political world, in that order. No one mentioned a teacher, a doctor, an artist, a writer, a musician, or anyone from the professional and cultural worlds. These were rather thoughtful children from above average homes.

These choices indicate the tremendous influence of the mass media. A radio and television hero came first. A scientist came next. Many were not sure who Einstein was, but his name was a symbol of science.

This discussion so interested this lecturer that she set up like situations in various schools over the country during the next two years in large cities, in small towns, in rural areas. The answers were always the same; some mass media hero *first,* Einstein second, and sports, military, political leaders next. But never a name from the cultural or professional world was suggested.

This is what is so, despite all the school's teaching of who the great people are. It should give us reason for thought. It would seem to indicate that the mass media actually are the most powerful teachers in our generation, developing the values and attitudes which truly dominate children's behavior.

Despite the frank facing of the poor quality of most television programming today, all the surveys made so far indicate that the average viewing time for children 10 to 15 years of age, is *four hours per day.* The longest viewing time per day is by the 12- to 14-year group. A recent study made for a master's thesis at Stanford University in Palo Alto, California of 1860 families owning television sets practically substantiates these figures. Of this total, nearly 100 homes owned two television sets because of family conflict of interests.

Many people have talked of the good results of television in keeping a family at home and giving them something to do together. But most of the parents reporting in this survey said that the television set ought to be in a separate room, not in the living room, that it created more problems than it solved.

Much of television's time goes to showing old movies of wide variance in interest or quality and putting on vaudeville shows of entertainment, also of wide variance in interest or quality. This is not to minimize the excellent showing of many sports such as football and baseball which satisfy the male members of the family; the excellent science programs such as Dr. Poole's Johns Hopkins Science Review, "Today's Science and You," and "Mr. Wizard"; and the unique school hour for pre-school children, "Ding Dong School," which is proving so helpful both to mothers and young children.

TV offers a steadily increasing number of good programs which stimulate excellent interests with which teachers and parents can and ought to build. Disneyland has a tremendous hold not only upon children but many adults. The programs on natural history in both TV and movies are excellent. The "Living Desert" and the "Vanishing Prairie" are also available in books with fine color photographs and accurate text. More are to follow. This can lead to further reading of the George Mason books, *Animal Travels, Animal Weapons, Animal Clothing,* and the others; the life cycle books, such as *Frogs and Toads, Homing Pigeons, Hamsters,* by Herbert Zim; the Mesaland Series about desert life such as *Cocky, Baby Jumping Jack Rabbit,* and others, by Lloyd S. Tireman; and *Nature's Ways,* by Roy Chapman Andrews.

Most children are interested in animals. Marlin Perkin's "Zoo Parade" is a good, live TV program. There is his book of the same title to read, other books about zoo animals, and, best of all in building real scientific understanding, Glenn Blough's *When You Go to the Zoo.*

Many historical characters such as Davy Crockett, Daniel Boone, and others are presented in a variety of programs. There are life stories of these men at a variety of reading levels with which to follow through. Let us take Davy Crockett and Daniel Boone as examples in reading ladders.

DAVY CROCKETT

			Grade level
Old Whirlwind	Coatsworth	Macmillan	3
Story of Davy Crockett	Meadowcroft	Grosset & Dunlap	5
Davy Crockett	Holbrook	Random House	6
Chanticleer of Wilderness Road	Le Seuer	Knopf	6
Yankee Thunder	Shapiro	Messner	6
Davy Crockett	Powers	Coward-McCann	7-8

DANIEL BOONE

			Grade level
Daniel Boone	Averill	Harper	3
On Indian Trails with Daniel Boone	Meadowcroft	Crowell	4
Story of Daniel Boone	Steele	Grosset & Dunlap	5
Daniel Boone	Brown	Random House	6-7

There are also characters from great literature being recreated in excellent dramatic form which arouse eager interest in children: Robin Hood, King Arthur, Peter Pan. Watching the fine presentations will send many a child to Pyle's *Robin Hood* or one of the many other good versions; to Pyle's *King Arthur* and also many other good versions; and to Barrie's delightful, imaginative story of Peter Pan.

The superb presentations of Shakespeare by Maurice Evans, Laurence Olivier, and others hold the interest of many children. It is of great help to prepare them for both seeing and hearing Shakespeare plays to read *The Wonderful Winter, Introducing Shakespeare,* and *Stories from Shakespeare* by Marchette Chute, as well as *Will Shakespeare and the Globe Theatre* by Anne Terry White. Shakespeare and the Globe Theatre become truly familiar to the reader.

It is not only possible in both interest and curricular terms, but valuable and important for teachers and parents to be fully aware of what TV offers that is worthwhile in science, history, geography, and literature, and to provide reading that capitalizes upon and builds with these excellent presentations.

The opportunity to see political conventions, United Nations meetings, and other important conferences in action is invaluable to the members of a democratic society which has grown as large as ours.

The possibilities of what television can present are wonderful. Every month sees improvement in programs. Educational television has great potentialities and may bring into home and school good programs of significant interest and quality. What the nature of both commercial and educational television is to be probably depends much upon the public and what it demands and supports as a viewing audience.

The reports from libraries on the influence of television upon reading are interesting. Most communities report a drop in circulation for the first two years following wide ownership of television sets. After that, most of them report an upswing in circulation. Some report a marked increase due to the stimulation of many interests and the desire to be better informed. Some report that both children and adults want to read the book from which a television show has been adapted and feel that actually television in the long run may encourage more reading.

We are in the embryonic stages of television development, but we cannot minimize the current influence of television upon our pattern of living, upon our values and attitudes, and upon our reading habits. What the nature of its future development will be, what place in total experience it is to have, depends largely upon what we do to exert influence upon its purveyors. Television is here to stay. Its characteristics as well as its power in the last analysis rests with us, the viewers.

Much of what is true of television is also true of radio. There are still a few areas in the United States where television has not developed. Radio is almost everywhere. The listening audience is still great, for adults and children have favorite programs to which they listen regularly. Wild cowboy adventures, exciting murder mysteries, and exotic space adventures constitute the bulk of the programs to which children listen. Cheap values, poor human relations, unwholesome presentation of crime, over-stimulation, and wild excitement characterize most of these programs. Both radio and television occupy some of a child's waking hours, part of which could well go to reading and outdoor play or other forms of activity. In many cases, children themselves, especially those 7 to 10 years of age, make their own adjustments. Norman, aged 7, said after three days with a new television set in the home, "This show is okay, but I wish Daddy would read some more of *Treasure Island* to me."

The late programs of both television and radio for which many children are allowed to stay up is reducing the amount of sleep they get, thereby harming the health of many children. The change in eating habits, such as eating from a tray while watching or listening to a show, or postponing regular eating hours is not good for children.

Radio and television in America are commercially sponsored. This means that children hear the praises of beer, toothpaste—all kinds of products—sung or expounded in terms that sometimes have little relation to truth. Few children have any background of actual knowledge from which to judge or evaluate these sales devices.

How is a child to learn facts with a flood of such statements filling his ears hours every day? The recent extravagant claims for chlorophyll are a striking example of a mixture of a little knowledge, a need for a new lure, and skillful propaganda. Richard spent many hours watching television. This fall he entered second grade, where the first unit of study centered around the farm. One day the class visited a dairy farm. When Richard came home he said, "Grandmother, you know all this stuff about chlorophyll? Well, it's all the bunk. I swallowed it whole and made Daddy buy chlorophyll toothpaste to make sure my breath never smelled bad. Those cows on the farm eat grass all the time. Grass is green and full of chlorophyll, but those cows smell awful."

It is difficult to overemphasize the tremendous influence of the commercials, the cheap values in some programs, the angles of emphasis (wrong is always punished, right wins out, but how?) upon today's child. It may well be that the school has to change many of its outmoded techniques, develop and use new ones in order to really teach a child today's pattern of life. The school competes with these media and today is on the losing side, chiefly because the mass media techniques are so successful. The content, then, becomes greatly confused in the child's mind, and what is inadequate, unfair—even untrue—sticks, essentially because the technique is so successful.

Most children, seven to ten years of age, love animals and subsequently love animal stories. Let a storyteller say he is going to tell a jungle story. The instantaneous response is terrific. If one asks why, heads pull down, voices take on an eerie quality as they answer, "Oo—oo. Because it's scary." It is Tarzan's jungle, not Kipling's, that is springing first into their minds.

The comics (so-called) are another powerful factor in American life today, both that of children and adults. Perhaps the high interest level of content with ease in reading may account for some of their popularity. But one cannot generalize in considering this material so beloved by so large a part of all American children from every economic bracket. One sees many parents, even intelligent ones, bring them home, buy them "to keep the children quiet or satisfied," as they say. The sight of a dozen or two children sitting around any supermarket absorbed in a comic while mother shops is too common to arouse comment any longer. Surveys show that many children read close to 100 different comics per week regularly. One newsstand in an Indiana town of about 5,000 population purchases 750 kinds each week, 10 each of the "just plain funny ones like Donald Duck," but 25 to 50 each of the thrillers, and sells out weekly. There are today about 1,300 kinds of those "un-comic non-books" as E. E. Cummings calls them, selling over 20 million copies a month.

Many studies of the wide reading of the comics and the effects upon children have been made by Sterling North, Paul Witty, Ruth Strang, and others. An excellent summary of the place of the comics is made by David Russell in *Children Learn to Read*, Houghton Mifflin, 1949, pp. 260-67.

Early in the 1900's comic strips began to appear in many newspapers in the form of long series of cartoons of certain characters that continued week after week poking fun at human foibles. As time went on, some of these stories became straight adventure yarns. Somehow, gradually the adventure became wilder and more thrilling, less and less related to real life. Actually, all comics do not fall into these three categories of fun, adventure, and thriller, for both humor and information may be found in many. Adventure and the extreme, thrilling, unreal, experience are in many others, often now with no humor. In discussing them it is advisable, therefore, to designate which group is being considered.

Of today's total, many of which still appear in strips in newspapers, about 20 per cent are still chiefly humorous, needling man's foibles, by animals like *Donald Duck* or children like *Dennis the Menace*. About 10 per cent are straight adventure yarns. About 10 per cent are "true" comics consisting of science stories in which scientific facts are associated with adventure, retelling of adventures selected from history, retelling of Bible stories, retelling of famous classics. The remaining 60 per cent are wildly exciting, unreal thrillers into which have entered pornographic interest, unethical concepts, fantastic presentation of criminals and crime, and many undesirable stereotypes.

Some people think that comic readers find a certain wish fulfillment in this last type of experience which affords a catharsis like that of the identification in certain dramatization. It is difficult to measure this value against all the undesirable elements. Ruth Strang[1] mentions this as a favorable argument as well as suggesting that comics offer the child of limited reading ability a form of satisfying reading experience and that they actually may extend the vocabulary of some children. Others say that some comics help develop a child's sense of humor, that the true comics present certain scientific facts and historic information in an "easy to understand" fashion which gains children's interest better than the duller presentation in the average textbook.

---

[1] Ruth Strang, "Why Children Read Comics," *Elementary School Journal*, Feb. 1943, Vol. 43, pp. 336-42.

In studies of certain groups of children's reaction to the true comics published by *Parents' Magazine,* the children said that these comics:

1. Presupposed too much background on the part of children.
2. Covered too much ground too fast. (The average comic takes one an impercetible distance from here to there, it is true, and demands, therefore, just that much gray matter for comprehension.)
3. Were too serious.
4. Were not exciting enough.

The undesirability of the unethical concepts of the 60 per cent mentioned above chiefly concerned with crime, sex, and unreality needs no extended consideration. The effect of continuous time given to such experience upon the development of a wholesome well-adjusted child is of serious concern. Besides the extremely undesirable values and the unreality, the art is inferior, the paper on which they are printed is hard on the eyes, the speech is often ungrammatical, and they seldom give a child anything like the feeling that reading good literature does. Much time spent with comics leaves little time for reading better things.

Reading comics and getting a story from these crude pictures of Robin Hood, King Arthur, David, and Samuel is not comparable to reading the story itself. A few teachers and librarians say the comic sometimes can be used as a lure leading into a better reading experience. There are a group of leaders, such as Josette Frank of the Child Study Association of New York, who say that we must meet the child where he is. Any reading is better than none. So let the child read whatever comics he wants to, and hope they lead him on to other things eventually.

What to do with the comics is obviously a complicated problem. Certainly it is important to help children evaluate them. It does not help to forbid them. The child who may not have them at home will get them from the child at school who secretly runs a rental library of comics out of his locker, or he can make the rounds of doctors' and dentists' waiting rooms. Status with one's peer group is dependent upon familiarity with today's adventure of Superman or Dick Tracy, so a child finds them somewhere and reads them.

Sometimes it is advisable to have children bring all their comics to a table in the classroom and discuss them openly, telling which ones they like and why. A science teacher once had his pupils bring in all the science comics they could collect and study them for accuracy. What accurate facts were learned in that process far exceeded any textbook lessons of comparable length.

The height of absorption in the comics seems to come during early adolescence, especially in seventh and eighth grades, for brighter children a little earlier. As more interests and more experience with interesting books, music, and art comes into their lives, there is less actual time for comics. They are chaff and what happens to chaff happens to the comics. In a good threshing job, the chaff falls to the ground, the wheat is kept. If there is enough wheat made available to the child, the chaff falls to the ground. So, in a lush environment, comics are seldom the all-absorbing interest.

Actually the comic technique is often a good one for quick communication of an idea. The army's use of a comic technique to teach reading to illiterate adults is ample proof of this. The comic problem is far more concerned with poor content, poor paper, and poor drawing than with the technique itself.

A first grader once said as he described a big balloon out of the corner of his mouth with his finger, "I like comics because you can always tell who says what. The chicken tracks in books (quote marks) aren't easy to follow." Maybe we live in more than one kind of balloon age!

Thus, there are many aspects, some favorable, more adverse, to the influence of comics on children's lives today. All the later discussion in this book may throw more light upon the whole problem and offer some helpful ideas both in analyzing the problem and finding what to do to help children and teachers and parents.

The fourth mass medium of great force in today's living is the movie. Many of the same kinds of values that characterize the other mass media characterize the movie. Too many of them are lurid, with unwholesome and unethical values and poor human relations. Of course there are some fine historical movies, some excellent dramatizations of great plays and great stories; but, the greatest quantity of films filling corner movies is not of this quality. And our children frequent the corner movie by the thousands. Many from homes where there is not much supervision or where parents work at night go two or three times a week. The sleepy child in school next morning is not a good learner. Fortunately, in many homes, movie attendance is restricted to the week end so that school nights give adequate time for sleep. The majority of American children see at least one movie a week, and the majority of those movies are not of a very high quality.

In a western movie, one of the most popular kinds, the villain is usually caught and killed. Movies lead children to think that a cowboy's chief occupation is riding over wild country on the hunt for a raider or rustler or villain of some kind, who then is trapped and killed. The production of such stereotypes and many others, most of them utterly untrue to real life, is unfortunate.

The constant excitement, thrilling adventure, real or imaginary, develops in children a constant demand for over-stimulation, excitement, thrills. Ordinary pastimes and occupations of normal, average living become far too dull and tame.

The opportunity for children, especially younger children, to see in detail adult experiences is often unwholesome. Television makes this even more intimate as the child watches pictures at close range. The ultimate results of such intimate observation of adult experience upon children may be far reaching and create many psychological and psychiatric problems.

But, some one will say, there are good educational movies, used in most of our schools today. Alas, not many are really good, or at least not good enough. Just listen to the adjectives children use in describing them—"punk," "dumb," "tame," "silly," and many more. Actually the movie and most audio-visual resources are not good enough and not well integrated with the school curriculum, *as yet*. Few teachers are really well enough trained in their use. It is hard to get that good film about Mexican life just when you are studying Mexico. Thus, the movie in the auditorium is too often just another show for the children— a change from the classroom, while for the teacher it is a rest! As a movie viewing experience it is poor by comparison with outside experience. It could be better, but it is not yet. It is not truly a satisfying resource, not really integrated into our teaching program.

The mass media are powerful influences in the lives of all of us in America—not all bad of course, but not enough that is good. Educational radio missed the boat, as we all know. What it could do, we also realize. Will educational television do likewise? We hope not. This very moment is education's golden opportunity to develop a television program of worth and significance. If only this could happen, it might well change the character and caliber of all the mass media. It is a tremendous challenge to each one of us to make our influence felt wherever any educational station is beginning, both in support and aid in the production of interesting, worthwhile programs that will satisfy our needs for humor, beauty, excitement, information, even inspiration. It could happen here, but not without us.

But realization of the power and influence of the mass media does not preclude adequate appreciation of the place of reading in today's living. As Marchette Chute said:

The mass media of communication can confer one great gift; they can place you in the center of things. But they cannot tell you how you got there or what you ought to do about it. They cannot confer perspective and they cannot help you to gain wisdom.

2 Marchette Chute, "Why Read Books?" *Scholastic Teacher,* Nov. 3, 1955, p. 2.

It is not *either/or*, but rather *both/and*. It may well be that children and adults of the next 100 years will read fewer words than most readers of today. Pictures and excellent graphs will convey vividly and briefly many ideas and much information. Long descriptions will not be needed and so will not be desired. The factor of time means that materials can be presented in a terse, brief, more direct fashion. But communication through words on the printed page is here to stay. No one can function *easily* in our society who cannot read direction signs, names of streets, roads, places, or labels on food and all the things we use.

Pete never really learned to read. By the time he was fifteen he had been pushed along to seventh grade, so they put him into eighth grade and graduated him at sixteen. He lived in a large city and knew only city life. He went out to find a job. He could not clerk in any kind of store because he could not read labels. He could not sell gas at a service station because he could not read labels or names. He could not deliver telegrams or packages because he could not read streets or names on the messages or packages. After two months of anxious searching, he found a job. He could help collect garbage, the only job in a big city that he could do well. But Pete did not want to collect garbage. So he returned to his favorite teacher and asked her to teach him to read.

"I'll learn this time. I know I will because I want to."

He did, too, in about five months of intensive work at a reading clinic.

But this should not happen to any child in America. If reading comes into a child's life easily and naturally when he begins to realize the need for communication beyond that of talking with his family and the people he associates with, he accepts the process and eagerly goes about mastering those symbols that can tell him about places, people, ideas from anywhere, at any time. If he can begin by finding out about something that interests him, he is much more likely to make the effort to discover what the symbols are. Also he is much more likely to gain satisfaction from the experience if he can get meaning from a whole sentence and several sentences rather than just learning separate words as words which may or may not be put together interestingly. A sixth grader was showing a new story book to two other boys in his room. "Know that word," he'd ask, pointing to a word. "No." "What's this one?" "Don't know." After a few minutes one of the "unknowing" ones flashed back, "Want to know something? Just knowing words ain't reading!"

This simplest use of reading, essential to just getting around easily in any American community, is its most elementary use. As such, it may indicate some first ways of beginning to teach reading by naming all the objects and places most commonly met in home and school, but that is never enough to hold a child's interest or give sufficient incentive for him to think reading will continue to be a rewarding and necessary activity for him.

Any person who is going to want to read must early discover other values. He must find out that it is one of the chief ways of getting needed information. It is not the only way, but at present it is one of the chief ways. Each individual who can read can find out anything that men who have lived before him have found out and go on from there. This is true in any area of knowledge—science, arithmetic, geography, history. He may want to make an experiment to see how a plant grows in water or in soil, and he learns much from firsthand experience; however, he cannot possibly experiment with everything that grows. So he reads what other men have found out. He may be able to go to the desert in Southern California or New Mexico, but not to the Sahara or Gobi; but he can read about the latter. It is necessary that a child discover early that reading is one of the many good ways to get the information he needs.

In a democracy, when there is true freedom of speech, anyone may write or say what he wishes. Hence, it becomes important to help children learn early what constitutes accurate factual information and what may be advertising or propaganda. The possession of information develops competency for his work and usefulness, but it must be accurate. The more he reads, the greater his experience, the more able he becomes in sifting knowledge and facts from propaganda or promotion statements —an important ability for every citizen in a democracy. Obviously, the good reader saves much time by his ability to get needed information quickly.

All human beings need change, rest, and relaxation for good health. Reading stories, adventures in other lands, lives of people who have done interesting things offer diversion and/or escape. The mystery story of today, with a sharp plot line and problem to be solved by one's wits, is a favorite form of reading for escape, even for many intellectual people in important positions. For the eight- to ten-year old, a good animal story often offers this escape. It later becomes adventure, mystery, or experience outside one's own environment. This value of reading for rest and relaxation—"getting away from it all"—is not to be considered lightly. If it becomes escape from reality, it may be unhealthy, but, as restful escape from the ordinary work and cares of life, it is a good thing.

This aspect leads us to think of another healthful psychological value of reading. Often it helps one to read a story or biography of a real person who is much like oneself. The strong resemblance makes possible an identification which may prove helpful in understanding oneself, in working out specific personal problems. Such identification through vicarious experiences may bring deep satisfaction to many readers. A shy child may feel much encouragement when he reads the life of Albert Einstein or Stephen Foster. The child who is self-conscious in a minority group may find just the understanding he needs when he reads *The Story of Jim Thorpe*, by Schoor, *Ralph J. Bunche*, by Kugelmass, or stories such as *The Hundred Dresses*, by Estes, *Bright April*, by De Angeli, *All American*, by Tunis, *Teresita*, by Means, *Palomino Boy*, by Emblen.

The handicapped child may feel happier, both in accepting

his handicap and overcoming it if possible, when he reads *Door in the Wall,* by De Angeli, or *Triumph Clear,* by Beim.

Thus, reading gives information which leads to knowledge which may lead to some wisdom; reading is a time saver; reading is relaxation; reading is fun; reading is adventure; reading is a problem solver; reading may be an aesthetic experience, as is listening to music or looking at pictures.

There is literature. There is poetry. Some writing is an art form capable of giving the highest aesthetic pleasure and satisfaction. A poem is more than the sum total of the meanings of the 65 words used therein. A folk tale or epic legend is more than the sum total of the 65 hundred words used in it. Words are more than symbols, more than meaning, more than sounds. Words have undertones and overtones. Words put together in beauty enter the mind and soul of man and take him literally "out of this world" into a realm of understanding or imagination or beauty or joy past believing. Thus, one may reach the very heights of aesthetic experience through reading poetry and some literature. The riches and variety of such possible experience are vast.

No audio-visual device discovered or undiscovered can ever give this experience. The mechanical brain may be able to answer many questions, but it cannot ask even one. As long as men speak and write, men will listen and read words put together to offer the highest aesthetic experience man's mind or spirit can comprehend. Children must sometimes be burdened with our current overwhelming emphasis upon getting the facts and piling up information. There is beauty. There is humor. There are the dreams beyond dreams which are children's heritage and opportunity.

No wonder we call reading a key—a key well worth using for utilitarian purposes or for transcendent experience as lofty as any that music may offer in the realm of sound and rhythm, or art in the realm of color, mass and line. Reading is a means of communication that transcends time and space, spiritual as well as physical.

BOOKS ARE MORE THAN WORDS[3]

Books are more than words
more than birds'
brightness, more than song,
They last long.
When the covers close
wisdom grows,
every thought is root,
leaf and fruit.
Every good page turned
is love learned.
—Joseph Joel Keith

[3] Permission granted by *The Saturday Review,* New York.

3

Factors Conditioning the Child Who Reads

*I*N discussing why people read—why they should read and are likely to read—we have been primarily concerned with the concept of reading and its function in living and learning in a democratic social order, with some analysis of the characteristics of our particular American democracy of the mid-twentieth century. It is necessary now to consider the child himself, some of his basic needs, and the circumstances under which he is likely to find reading one of the good resources for his own living and learning.

Mass reading is no more possible than mass learning. Equal opportunity for learning does not mean identical opportunity. The children in any fifth grade have as many differences as likenesses. Each child is an individual with his own developmental pattern of growth; this means that each learns in his own way, not in someone else's. No Tom can be Dick; no Dick can be Harry; no Harry can be Tom: *each must be himself.* The rate of growth is different for each child. No two children aged six years and three months are alike in their levels of development. Individuals differ and the sexes differ. Insufficient recognition and acceptance of this wide divergence in growth patterns exists in far too many primary and elementary classrooms. The only really adequate learning situation for any child is one in which he can really learn in his own way and at his own rate of speed. This does not mean that every room has 35 different individuals all doing different things at the same time. But it also does not mean that the 35 all do the same thing at the same time. The necessity for finding what can be done as a whole group, what can be done in small groups, and what must be done individually probably is the most difficult task any teacher has. But it is not an impossible task. It is truly challenging.

This is not a book on method, but it may help to explain certain techniques which have been of worth in handling problems posed by individual differences and individual growth patterns. Much pupil-teacher planning helps; some pupil-pupil planning is of value. A room with several centers of interest and adequate work space is best for the most satisfying learning situations in all grades, not just the primary grades. This means a reading corner with tables and benches or chairs of the right height, much shelf space, and *plenty of books.* Every day should have some time when each child is free to go to that reading center to read what he can and wants to read, at his own level of ability. His reading ability is an individual ability, dependent upon his mental equipment and heritage, certain aptitudes, his emotional stability, his experience, his family background and total socio-economic background.

Some people feel that mental ability is measurable and find IQ (Intelligent Quotient) tests valuable. Early users of Binet tests felt they were infallible, that results had little or no relation to socio-economic background or environment, that no change in IQ took place with growth, or could take place. Recent psychological research tends to modify this certainty. Certainly the mental equipment of human beings differs widely. The "smart" child is much more likely to read easily, to want to read intensively, than the child with less mental equipment. So, we must accept the fact that each child's reading ability will be different from every other child's, depending on the mental equipment and social experience he brings to it.

There are also an increasing number of aptitude tests, some of which are helpful. This is a musical child; another is artistic. Some children have the love of detail that makes good research personnel. A forthgoing child, concerned about others' welfare, may make a good social worker, while one who is shrewd, "just like his father," may become a good businessman. Still another child's reasoning ability may make him a good lawyer. There are certain aptitudes, tendencies, and characteristics which are very likely to influence both the amount and type of reading he does.

An individual who works best with his hands is likely to do less reading. A musical child gives more time to playing an instrument, but may find his reading skill helps him read music more easily. He also may find that reading about musicians and types of music helps him understand and interpret better the music he wants to play. If he goes on into the study of harmony and counterpoint, he may spend more time actually reading in those areas than with music itself during certain periods in his growth. These various aptitudes have strong influences upon what a child does and upon the amount of his reading.

Children's emotional stability depends upon their individual physical and psychological characteristics, background, and many kinds of experiences. One child may be shy or definitely introverted, and thus may read a great deal to occupy himself when alone. He may read for escape. Shyness may block him early in life so that he never feels quite at ease with this new medium, or withdrawal due to introversion may be so great that he even avoids stories of people.

The child's mother may be a great reader. He early feels that books are his greatest competitor for her attention, so he resents them. He does not want anything to do with books, therefore, he will not learn to read. Perhaps the mother and father read to the child a great deal. He loves it, he begs for more, he has vicarious experience far beyond his age level. Or, he may just enjoy his parents' enjoyment. He reaches school and is eager to read, since he has enjoyed sharing his parents' reading. But it is such a slow process. The subject matter is so "dumb."

Thus, it frequently happens that a child who has had fairy tales, folk tales, and pioneer adventures read to him evening after evening is bored and impatient with a process which offers him a few words which really have nothing to say to him. It is interesting to note how many elementary schools, located near colleges and universities or in sections where most of the parents are college graduates, report that many children show this boredom and lack of interest and resultant lack of willingness to exert any effort to learn to read.

Douglas' grandmother is a distinguished author. His father writes well in his professional field. Douglas belongs to a highly intelligent, cultured, reading family. His teacher hesitated to report his lack of interest in reading, his persistent refusal to try to read any primer offered to him. His grandmother realized what was happening and tried to talk with him about it. Douglas said,

"You should see what they expect me to read. They're not

books. No one really talks the way they do in those school books. It's so silly I can't be a part of it."

Here was an intelligent child with a serious block. One day his teacher thought she might capitalize on his devotion to his father and his fondness for dogs. So she chose a primer in which a dog played with the children and said: "Douglas, wouldn't you like to take this home and read it to your father?"

Douglas looked at her and said very courteously, "Would you like to take it home to read to your father? Neither would I."

On the other hand, many children never see any reading occur in their homes and therefore feel it is not a part of real living. Occasionally a child has had to live with prolonged illness of a loved member of his family who reads much of the time. The association of reading with illness gives the child an emotional block which results in definite aversion. Sometimes a child who is used to excelling has difficulty in visualizing words and carrying the image from one day to the next. He is so ashamed of his inability that he tries to hide it by memorizing a page or using other schemes until the inevitable time comes when the truth about his word recognition is evident. He become more ashamed and refuses to make any effort, saying to himself that this is something he just cannot do. He can do other things and will compensate by excelling in those.

Many other instances could be cited of emotional and psychological experiences which so condition a child that he refuses to exert himself to learn to read. Once slow at it, he remains slow and therefore derives little real satisfaction from reading. Such experiences happen to mentally superior, average, and below average children. Often, a school psychologist and understanding parents can help in removing such blocks, especially if happier associations can be made to replace the unhappy associations.

Lastly, there are a few physical handicaps that may limit a child's reading ability. His eye span may be shorter than average. His eye focussing may not be exact, so that there is a blur on the edge of letters. He may be a mirror reader and see all letters backward, both in shape and in order. He may not make slight distinctions easily, so that *m* and *w*, *n* and *u*, *p* and *b* are hard to learn as distinct letters. It is usually fairly easy to discover physical disabilities like these and to correct them.

No child is ever going to read much if he does not gain satisfaction from reading. It must be fairly easy to follow words, lines, and paragraphs, to turn pages quickly to get at what comes next, otherwise, the child will choose some other experience. His reading much or little is clearly dependent upon his ability to read whatever is likely to appeal to his own age level. One Tommy is eager to read "Run, Tommy, Run." Another Tommy is not ready to read "Run, Tommy, Run." And Susie is ready to read about flying an airplane.

One or two other reminders in thinking of each individual learner may be helpful in our thinking. Each level of development is not necessarily a separate stage, easily separated and distinguished from the previous level. Also, the growth characteristics overlap, further complicating each individual's pattern. This means that a good teacher needs to study each child's developmental pattern so that the best learning situations may be planned for him. The results from this extra effort will far exceed the effort involved.

Children do not learn to do any task by being required to do one of which they are not yet capable; they learn only failure. They learn only by doing what they can do, succeeding in that and going on from there to the next successful accomplishment. Giving a failing mark usually means only that the teacher is requiring of Johnny achievements for which he is not yet ready. If a classroom learning situation is not flexible enough or set up in terms of helping Johnny learn what he is ready to learn and needs to learn for his own best growth, then he belongs somewhere else. Spending two years in this same room is not likely to be of much value to him. This is particularly true in the area of reading for learning, which is sometimes retarded by learning to read.

There is much current discussion about the way in which reading is taught today. Of course it is different from the way it was taught 50 or even 25 years ago. Phonics has come, gone, returned, found a place. Views on just when to learn the alphabet vary. There is some divergence of opinion on the relative importance of skill in word recognition and on the need for interest. The way in which we teach many subjects is different today. We teach manuscript writing in the first and second grades, changing to cursive writing at about the age of eight because we know a little more about large and fine muscle growth, use, and adjustment. Our teaching of arithmetic also differs, its vital concern being to teach the meanings of arithmetical concepts rather than just having children learn number combinations by rote memory.

With the growth of biology, physiology, psychology, and anthropology, we actually know more about how a child grows and learns. Thus, most schools are much more concerned, both in curriculum planning and in evaluation of the child's learnings, with a child-development point of view.

The so-called "word" method of teaching reading involves much phonics when taught by a good teacher. In attacking new words, a child helps himself by thinking how the word begins, by looking for a part he knows in a word or a little word in a big word, by thinking how the word ends, by using the sense of the whole sentence to help him with the word, and by getting a picture of the general shape of the word. A child's interests are used actively by a good teacher to develop his reading skill and his desire to read.

Research in child development is extensive these days, and constant new light and understanding is given to us through books and education journals. Some of the facts presented only sum up what we know so far. It behooves all teachers, school administrators, and school boards to try to set up school

Curry School, Women's College, University of North Carolina

Karen likes to read.

Reading is of interest to child, mother, and teacher.

1 B. Campbell, Public Schools, Altoona, Pa.

Lindenwood Elementary School, Norfolk, Va.

It helps to know the ropes.

Reading aloud is fun.

Mary Caicott School, Norfolk, Va.

situations in terms of what we do know about children's development and their ways of learning, and to keep an open mind about what we may learn in the future. Only in this manner have we any right to be working with children. Every teacher needs to accept the fact that children's individual abilities inevitably determine their reading ability.

Certain basic needs of all children in general are accepted by educators today. Dr. Louis E. Raths of the education department of New York University summarizes these needs as follows:[1]

1. In order to feel good about his life every child has to have some sense of *belonging*.

2. The feeling of worth each of us has, if we are to become sure of ourselves, must be moved again and again by *achieving*.

3. *Economic security* seems to be a continuity of that which has sustained life in a warm and trusting relationship.

4. *Freedom from fear*. When children begin to learn how to handle "fearful" situations by cautious approaches, by preparation and readiness, they are also being helped to handle their fears and to make their inner life more secure.

5. The *longing for love and affection* and for a deep and abiding trust in human relationships seems to be one of the most important needs. It is closely related to the need to belong.

6. The basis of good human relations is self-respect. Children need to be *relatively free from guilt*. The development or prevention of intense feelings of guilt in a child depends to a great extent on whether he is judged by adult standards that he does not understand or judged by his own standards.

7. *Need for self-respect*. This feeling of personal worth that is built up in the early years of childhood is evidently of great importance in developing his healthy personality.

In our teaching we sometimes emphasize out of all proportion the place that information has in school life. Learning information is one thing. Learning to think and plan together, learning to identify values, learning to relate ourselves to other human beings in a friendly way, learning to appreciate differences, learning good habits of health, learning to explore the world are additional facets of total living. Giving children choices to learn these things is showing respect for their personalities.

[1] Louis E. Raths, *Do's and Don't's of the Needs Theory* (New York: Modern Education Service, 1951).

8. *Need for guiding purposes.* A child seeks direction for himself. Our job is to help him on the path so that he may more intelligently fashion his own purposes as he comes to understand the world.

May Hill Arbuthnot, formerly of Western Reserve University, gives seven such basic needs.[2] Hers are probably chosen with the thought of what needs books may satisfy rather than the more general psychological needs of Dr. Raths' choice.

1. The need for security—material, emotional, and spiritual.
2. The need to belong (to family, school, any group of which the child is part).
3. The need to love and be loved.
4. The need to achieve, to do or be something worthy.
5. The need to know in order to have intellectual security.
6. The need for change as exemplified in play, recreation; something to satisfy the sense of humor.
7. The need for aesthetic satisfaction.

Her first four are identical with Dr. Raths' first four, with a slight change in order having no special significance. Her fifth need is probably included in Dr. Raths' seventh. It is interesting to note that Dr. Raths feels it important to balance this need with others and not to get the acquiring of information out of balance in our values or set it up as an end in itself. Many school people need this angle of adjustment in their thinking. One often hears someone say of a teacher, especially a high school teacher, "Oh, he's a subject matter teacher. He knows his geometry, but he doesn't know kids." When a teacher conceives of his job as one of handing out information, there is reason to wonder how much actual teaching and learning takes place in his classroom. Does he know that anyone—his pupils, himself—learns only what he lives?

The sixth need—the need for change, rest, relaxation and fun —is surely one which is necessary for good health, for the de-

[2] May Hill Arbuthnot, *Children and Books* (Chicago: Scott, Foresman and Company, 1947).

velopment of objectivity, for the development of a balance in values. Like most proverbs, "All work and no play makes Jack a dull boy," evolved from much experience and a basic, sound common sense about human experience.

The seventh need concerns not only highly developed man. A love of beauty seems common to all mankind. Even primitive man adorned himself, those he loved, and his home. The full development of this sense and fulfilling the need it creates builds taste, discrimination, and becomes a distinctive characteristic of man at his highest level of cultural development.

A child's interests are as wide as the world. They begin with himself. The day a baby first discovers his toes is a big day for him. His interest soon includes himself, objects around him, other children, animals, plants, trees, rocks, stars, and the heavens. This is his world, and he wants to know all he can about it. He particularly wants to know what seems related to himself, his needs, his interests, and his characteristics, so that he can feel happy, useful, and adjusted.

Certain interests are stronger at certain times, but they often overlap even to the extent of causing confusion. Those interests are the guide posts for his activities, even as the basic needs are the groundwork and frame of the house of life a child builds. He begins in intimate personal terms, slowly but surely expanding to the wider, general terms that make him at home in his universe as well as in his own body.

The child who grows only into a self-centered human being is seldom a happy, adjusted person. The normal pattern of growth is from *self-centeredness* to *other-centeredness*, from a *human* being to a *humane* being. This is a slow, creative, dynamic process of growth, not an assembly line, mass production procedure. Even as it demands all the sensitivity, awareness, and insight possible for the grower, it demands these same qualities in the guide of these growing individuals.

No motivation for any human activity, therefore, can possibly be as strong as that of a child's basic needs and ever widening interests. The business of life is satisfying these, hence, they are the power drives that make the human organism work and grow. Since a human being is not just a machine, they must be dynamic, flexible, and adaptable to change, for they are living, organic, widely varying forms which the child uses, bends, molds to fit those needs and interests.

Reading about this world and its people, ideas, and ideals is inevitably one of the richest resources for meeting these needs and interests. When the process is easy, the nourishment enters his mind even as food is transformed in the blood stream into energy for the body. Such intellectual and spiritual nourishment is surely as valuable as physical nourishment, if not more so, hence, the importance of keeping the process an easy and happy experience.

It is important here for any and every teacher to realize that unless she herself is one for whom reading is a rich resource for her own living, it is not likely to be so for the children who live with her. Children are great imitators; they learn much through imitation. As the teacher is, so are her students. Changes in behavior of many children as they go from fourth grade to fifth grade attest this fact every day.

Teachers! All of you! Take a good look (as if you were a visitor from Mars) at your desk, at your room. Stand at that open door for a minute and look around and evaluate what you see. Would this visitor, seeing it all for the first time and trying to interpret what the things and their arrangement mean, think, "Ha, this is a person who loves to read, who also loves beauty. How charming that arrangement is on his desk. What simplicity! How right that blue of the low bowl is against the deep red-brown of the desk!

"What interesting books! Look at all those titles on his shelves! These few on his desk indicate that he must love some more than others. He likes poetry. Here on the desk is Robert Frost and *My Poetry Book*. On the shelves? Yes, one whole shelf is just poetry: De La Mare, Rossetti, Kipling, Noyes, Keats, Shelley, Emily Dickinson, Edna Millay, Robert Frost, Walt Whitman. His children will soon tell me which are good! "He likes people. There are so many books about real people: John James Audubon, Abraham Lincoln, Leif Ericson, Benjamin Franklin, George Washington Carver, Albert Schweitzer, Florence Nightingale, Wolfgang Amadeus Mozart, Ludwig van Beethoven, George Gershwin. Wonder who they were and what they did on this earth?"

Or will the visitor see a desk with an old blotter pad with irregular edges, a well-worn dictionary and two or three textbooks in dull gray bindings, leaning against each other, a pile of papers awaiting correction, and shelves not very full except for rows of old sets of textbooks, the backs so loose that threads are hanging? Can there be treasure in such ugly, outside wrappings? If there is, do they tempt the pupils in this room to look inside to find out? The visitor is not likely to think that the teacher in this room has any interest in reading; he is hard put to it to guess what his interests are.

Do your desk and your shelves make any child feel that you are an eager reader, that you find joy and satisfaction in many kinds of books? If he knows how much reading means to you, a teacher he admires, he is much more likely to want a like resource for himself. Actually, the measure to which reading satisfies your needs and interests is a factor in the children's attitude toward reading and their willingness to find in it a resource for themselves.

Parents, too! Does a visitor to your home know you love to read? Certainly the accessibility of books, magazines, and newspapers makes a great difference in whether or not children read. There should be a large quantity of these about every conceivable interest, at many levels of readability, easily available if children want to read. A child must be able to find a book he can read about something in which he is really interested, or he will pay no attention to books. The books must be where he can get at them easily, where there is wide selection of books which really look alluring.

Educators today talk about a lush environment if good learning is to take place. Children, at home and at schools, need a lush environment of books. There are more good readers and fewer reading problems in schools with a large number of carefully selected books. This fact is constantly confirmed by school surveys.

Whether the books are housed in a central library or in room libraries is a matter of mechanics and personnel. Some record should be kept of the books owned by a school. Children from four grades have a possible interest in a given book such as *Little House in the Big Woods.* If there is only one copy, belonging in one room library, the other three do not have much access to the book. In a central library, all grades have access to it, and records are likely to be better. But having books should not be dependent upon mechanics of administration.

Few elementary schools have trained librarians or are likely to have them in the near future. But one teacher might be released for a half day once a week to work with a library club of interested upper grade children. Parents are usually much concerned about their children's reading. The national P.T.A. has a strong section interested in children's books and reading. The book or library chairman might organize a committee to work with such a library club. Such a group can have fun accessioning and taking care of the books. Often they can do most of what is needed to really take care of the books.

Few books should ever be on the shelves in a functioning library or any place where books are housed in the school. They should be out—in use—and they will be, if they are right for the children. The important thing is to have plenty of books and to have them easily and freely accessible. The actual mechanics of care and distribution may differ widely and may be worked out in terms of space, time, and people willing to work. It is unfortunate for any school to wait to acquire many good books until highly professional arrangements can be made for their care and distribution. Start with getting books and children together as much as conditions allow. Mechanics improve with growth. Don't be afraid of simple beginnings. If the only feasible way at first seems to be having books in classrooms, have them there and encourage rooms to exchange books so that many children have access to them.

One hears, "But there is no money in our budget for books, except textbooks and a few reference books." This is, alas, too true in many places. But it is less and less true. The day is coming when every school budget will carry a book allotment as surely as it carries equipment and salary allotments. As administrators and school boards realize the necessity of providing books for adequate learning and for holding a child's interest and keeping him working, they will include such an item in all budgets.

In some cases, this realization comes slowly. Often a P.T.A. stimulates the interest and appropriates the first $100. Money-raising is not the function of the P.T.A., but much playground equipment, stage equipment, audio-visual equipment, books, and records are given by a P.T.A. because parents want their children to have the needed resources at school.

Some say books are expensive, but the cost of all living has increased. Food is expensive, clothes are expensive, shoes are expensive. It costs more to produce all goods, including books, so they, also, are expensive. But, too expensive for *what* or for *whom?* The figures on national expenditure for comics or chewing gum far exceed those for books. Is there a price on the good we want for our children? Many families cannot afford to buy as many books as the children need for good reading. They live far from the nearest public library, which often has only a small children's shelf, or one copy of a book when there ought to be five for the area being served. It is good for a child to own a few special books to love and cherish, but few families can afford to purchase as many books as growing children with wide needs and interests ought to have.

The one place where every child may have access to books is the school he attends. In today's pattern of education, it is logical to have this big resource easily available in the school where a child spends five of his waking hours every day. If this were the situation generally, teaching reading would be more a flourishing resource than a bewildering problem.

One hears frequently, "Of course, my children would read if they had any good books, if they had anything they really wanted to read." Many parents become greatly concerned over the amount of time spent by their children with comics. They get highly worked up over the values their children are acquiring from the comics. So, the teacher or visiting speaker suggests that this reading is done to satisfy their children's eagerness for fun and adventure and asks, "What really humorous books are there in your home?" "What good adventure tales are there?" "Does the family ever read these aloud together?" The invariable answer is an embarrassed admission of "None," or "A couple." If the chaff is cheap and easily accessible or is all that is accessible, the child is not to blame for knowing only chaff. If he has access to some wheat also, he usually finds it both more palatable and nourishing, and wants it, instead. Book fairs and hobby shows may raise money to purchase books. Gradually, as records show higher reading levels in achievement tests in schools with many books, the teachers, school boards, and communities realize the value of having many good books easily available.

One teacher and a few parents in an Illinois town were concerned over the lack of any interest in reading. There was no real bookstore in town and a rather limited children's bookshelf in the public library. One fall, in early November just before Book Week, these parents in cooperation with a bookseller in a nearby city held a book fair at which children, parents, and friends looked at books and bought them. These parents sold

$692 worth of books, of which sum they kept 20 per cent. With the $138.40 they bought some of the books in which the children showed interest.

At a meeting of the eighteen elementary school principals of this town the following June, the superintendent reported that the children of the school which had held the book fair showed a higher rate of increase in reading level from the previous year and also passed reading tests and achievement tests at a higher level than any school in the town.

That was twelve years ago. The school still holds an annual book fair; so do many of the other schools in the town. The state school librarian considers this school library one of the best in the state. One interesting feature of every year's fair is that the children put slips in the books they want purchased for the school library. Some books must have a box with the book's name on it to hold the slips. Much thought and interest go into this job of selection.

One year, the total cost of the books selected came to more than the amount earned from the fair, so the principal said to the library club acting as a committee on this project, "We do not have enough money to buy as many books as were selected. We will have to take out some."

"Why, Miss M., we can't take any out. We have to have those books, we can't live without them. Honestly! We just have to find a way to earn a little more money. That's easy."

It must have been "easy," for they got the books.

Not only is this school library a good one, but many children have started small libraries of their own. There are books in most of the homes of this town. There is also a good book store and quite extensive book departments in two other stores. The library circulation has increased so that the appropriation for book purchases is larger. Reading has become a rich resource for living and learning in this small city. It is just an average community. The school where all this started is in a section where incomes are modest, but where most families own their own small homes. These people are interested in their children. They have discovered what books can mean for themselves and their children.

One day at a fair about two years after this, a sixth grade teacher came visiting from a nearby town. She became enthusiastic about the idea and its possibilities. So, her school held a fair the next fall with results that made both children and parents happy. A few years later, her superintendent asked her to become principal of a small school at the edge of town, serving a community of people who worked in a large dairy plant and other nearby industries. The building was very old and ugly—one of those old brick buildings with two rooms on the first floor and two on the second. Such proportions! But the children were dear, so this teacher accepted the job with one condition.

"Will you promise to give me $500 for books, good books for these children to read in addition to textbooks? Few of them have any books at home, and I have seen what it can mean to have plenty of books easily available at school."

The superintendent wanted her, so he agreed, grumbling a little over how he could ever get an extra $500.

There was a little square hall in the middle of that second floor. The new principal asked the sixth grade boys to help her build shelves for two sides of this hall, four shelves on each side, the full length of fifteen feet. The girls helped paint the shelves.

"What are these pretty new shelves for?"

"For our books," answered the new principal.

"But we keep our books in our desks," the children replied.

"Not these new books. Next week nearly 500 new books— picture books, story books, books about birds, books about stars, poetry books, everything you can think of—will be here. Meanwhile, we want to organize a library club to help us take care of the books, put cards in them on which you can write your names when you take the books home to read."

Books, so many books to take home as well as to read at school! It was hard to keep the whole school from becoming the library club, but finally it started with twenty-five fifth and sixth graders.

The books came! Such treasure! Such excitement! The children read, wanted to read as never before in their lives. That fall they, too, held a book fair. Many homes owned a book for the first time.

The principal suggested one day that some of the children write to a favorite author. Many of them did. Succeeding falls brought some of the authors living in or near Chicago to this school's book fair. The principal took groups of the children into Chicago to participate in N.B.C.'s radio program, "Carnival of Books." They came to know more and more authors.

Jim Kjelgaard, who wrote *Big Red, Snow Dog,* and many animal stories, was a greatly beloved author. Several children corresponded with him. Then, one day, a sixth grade boy became ill; it turned out to be polio. His dog was killed by a passing car while he was away in the hospital. Mr. Kjelgaard's letters helped him get well. It was a great day, not only for the boy, but for the school and whole community when Mr. Kjelgaard came to town and gave this lad, now on the road to recovery, one of his fine shepherd dogs.

Such rich friendships, such widened horizons as books have brought to this community—all because of a principal who loved books.

Some people exclaim at the size and beauty of the library of the new school building they are entering this fall, but any child in the school or any parent in the community will tell you, "This had to be the best room in our school. It is the place for our books. You know how much we love books. Everyone does in our school."

It *did* happen here. It *can* happen anywhere. There are many ways to make it happen; these two worked in their respective communities. Other methods may be more suitable in other communities. All it needs is someone who has discovered what books can mean for living and learning and who cares that children shall make that discovery for themselves, thus having the chance to live in a situation offering this rich resource.

4

Changing Concepts In Meeting Children's Needs and Interests

*B*ECAUSE so much depends upon the child's first reading experiences, this is one of the most critical
moments in his growing experience. A wrong start, an unhappy
association, may make a tremendous difference in a child's
whole life.

It will help our thinking to try to understand some of the
physiological and psychological characteristics of the average
six-year-old child.

He is at the beginning of that stage of lengthening out, of losing most of his baby roundness, in a period usually of fairly rapid growth. Since he is losing his first teeth, lisping and speech troubles sometimes appear. He is still at the stage of free use of large muscles. Painting at an easel or on a large sheet of paper on the floor is easier than on a small paper at a desk. He is just beginning to make the transition to a surer coordination of finer muscles. If this is not yet made, it is hard to hold a pencil or to focus the eyes on small print on a small page. It is very important to know the child's stage of large and small muscle coordination in order to make sure he does what he is ready to do. He is awkward and stumbles easily. He still needs plenty of rest, including a quiet period at least once, better still, twice, during the day.

This first experience of coming forth from the security of his home, where frequently his desires are paramount, into a world of competition with others like himself is not always pleasant. He is still self-centered. So are all the other first graders. He has to learn how to cooperate, and that is a slow process, and the advantages are not always quickly apparent to him. A few children enjoy being on their own, but many children have had so much help and care during the first six years of their lives that this sudden change demanding independence is not a happy time. This is why children in a large family or children of working mothers often make the first school adjustments easily because they are used to looking after themselves.

Most six-year-olds engage in individual activities, if given a choice, and make the change to becoming part of a group slowly. Conversation usually starts with "I" or "my." They are still "I-centered" human beings, full of energy and eager curiosity. Next to themselves, their greatest interest is in familiar animals; a little later, in all animals. Since this is a stage of almost "pure act," they are interested in everything that moves or goes; cars, steam shovels, tractors, trains, engines, airplanes—jets! The amount of information about rockets and jets which many six-year-old boys have today is amazing. An intelligent mother, genuinely concerned over her bright seven-year-old son's lack of interest in reading, recently said to an editor, "When will there be interesting stories of jets and planes that first graders can read? Your reading material has to be about their interests if it is to hold their attention and evoke a desire to read more. Airplanes, jets, and rockets are the strongest interests of all the small boys I know."

This situation poses a real problem, for most readers in basal series begin with 9 commonly used words, advance to 16, then to 27, and finally attain 250 words by the second grade; none of these concern jets or airplanes. If we honestly believe that children learn only what they live, then we must create living situations in which they have experience with meaning to bring about adequate learning. This applies to reading as well as to all areas of learning.

We talk about continuous learning a great deal these days. The child under six learns from his body, from looking at and handling every movable object in the world around him. He is motivated by all these sensory experiences to "read" the meaning of each thing. He *knows* many objects, "knows about" many more, but is not yet interested in ideas. Actually, the concept of obedience has little real meaning for him as yet, except that it is a good way to get what he wants and seems to make his parents, whom he loves and depends upon, happy. His greatest interest is in *things*, all the concrete things he can see and feel, both animate and inanimate.

Upon entering school, he used to be expected to sit quietly and be told about things, very soon to learn words on a page, and finally to read about things. This is not true in a good first grade room today, but there are "hangovers" in many, many schools. The transition is much too sudden from direct handling to reading about things, and does not form a continuous pattern of learning to extend gradually his preschool living. Actually he has a large oral and recognition vocabulary. Studies vary in their estimates from 2,500 to nearly 25,000. Madorah E. Smith[1] gauged 2,562 words for a six-year-old in her study made in Iowa in 1926. Robert H. Seashore and L. D. Eckerson,[2] a few years later, calculated 5,000 to 6,000 in their study which extended over ten years and was made in widely diverse areas of the entire United States, including urban and rural areas, industrial areas, and mining regions. They worked with children from all economic brackets. Mary K. Smith[3] in 1941 reported an average vocabulary of over 23,000 words in first grade children.

In any case, there is no doubt that the oral and recognition vocabulary of most six-year-olds is not in the hundreds but in the thousands, and in 1960 likely to be higher than in 1940 or 1941. Children of today, through television and radio, have access to experience far beyond that of the early 1940's. To satisfy such extensive interests as one moves from the recognition or hearing vocabulary—the stage at which a child understands the meaning of the words which he hears—to a reading vocabulary—the understanding of words which he sees on a printed page—poses a challenging problem which current reading procedures do not meet adequately. It has been generally assumed in most curriculum planning that most six-year-olds are ready to read. It could be that the great disparity between hearing and reading vocabulary, if we are willing to accept this extensive vocabulary as one indication of breadth of interests, is one important factor in the increasing reading difficulties of the present time.

[1] Madorah E. Smith, "An Investigation of the Development of the Sentence and Extent of Vocabulary in Young Children," *University of Iowa Studies in Child Welfare*, 1926, Vol. III, No. 5.

[2] Robert H. Seashore and L. D. Eckerson, "The Measurement of Individual Differences in General English Vocabularies," *Journal of Educational Psychology*, January 1940, Vol. 31.

[3] Mary K. Smith, "Measurement of the Size of General English Vocabulary through the Elementary Grades and High School," *Journal of Educational Psychology*, January 1941, Vol. 31.

When is a child ready to read? We say a child walks when he is ready, that is, when his muscle control, his coordination, his sense of balance, and his sense of direction enable him to move as an upright being rather than on all fours. The moment of such coordination varies widely in human beings, occurring often as early as nine or ten months and often as late as twenty-one or twenty-two months. He derives two kinds of satisfaction from his walking; the sense of his own personal achievement, and the evident approval of all the human beings around him. So, the experience satisfies at least two basic needs—that for achievement and that for being loved. It may even be a first stage of satisfying a third one, the need for change!

Talking also takes place when certain elements coordinate. This begins also at varying ages. It differs from walking in that it begins in a very simple, crude form which rapidly develops through use as all the satisfactions of communication become evident. The need for communication with someone not in his presence, the need for knowing about something he cannot see in his own room or home or school must have something to do with his readiness to read. Reading, and writing a little later, are both extensions of a child's early language abilities, usually occurring at a definite period in his intellectual development. Both are developed at a definite point in his physical maturation pattern when he is making the transition from large muscle control to control of the finer muscles.

Many textbooks on how to teach children to read discuss the whole question of reading readiness—what it is and how to recognize it, and what to do to build both on and with it. Thus, it does not seem necessary to present such discussion here. Careful observation of many children indicates that there is wide variation in the time at which this type of maturation takes place. Sometimes it happens in children as young as four years old, sometimes as late as eight. This fact suggests that a uniform treatment of six-year-olds is not a sure way of successfully teaching children to read. Here are a few considerations that may prove of value to the teacher who is anxious to find real understanding and help, and who is willing to open her mind to new ways and means in teaching.

The appearance of the printed page first given to a child beginning to read and the content and use of additional material and devices deserve serious consideration and should challenge teachers to far more experimentation. If there were more reports from teachers and children who have achieved satisfying and encouraging results, better teaching of six- and seven-year-olds might happen in more places. There are some first grades—not all in new schools or upper income bracket suburbs—from which, during the last five years, 75 per cent of the children go into second grade with reading abilities at the third grade level. Needless to say, those children also like to read. Here, then, are some ideas about the actual appearance of the page, the content, and some less conventional procedures.

The appearance of the first printed pages offered to a child has significance far beyond that we generally give to it. Most primers are printed in 18-point type. Sometimes, type as large as 24-point is used in preprimers. Nearly always it is some form of type with seraphs on the letters. It is, of course, close to the form which children will meet in books thereafter, but it is not in line with the letters the child has met before. Most children's first experience with letters grouped into words having meaning to him is in looking at signs, e.g., S T O P, G O, and R. R. X. Probably it is the red light which he first learns the meaning of. However, seeing the word with the red light usually means that he associates the word STOP with a red light, at the same time learning that word. The same is true of the green light and GO. Also, with gas station signs, railroad crossings, *Men* and *Women* on lavatory doors, and the more common store and market signs on every street. Now, most of those letters are not in Gothic or any fancy type. They are in plain letters in the basic shape of the letters used. S is just a curve with no frills or tails. *T* is one line across the top of another; *O* is a simple circle. *P* is a half circle on the right side of the upper portion of a straight line.

Some people think it is not important to teach the alphabet today. But one cannot be quite sure that this tendency is not toward "throwing out the baby with the bath." Most children are greatly interested in individual letters. "Old fashioned" grandparents and parents often teach letters as well as numbers to their children. They take great pride in the child who "knows his letters and his numbers," a pride the child quickly shares. Many a child still receives some kind of alphabet book before he goes to school, and he finds the letters and their pictures interesting. Most teachers teach the name and form of individual letters, although rote mastery of the letters is not considered as important for six- or seven-year-olds.

Last August, a group of boys, aged 5½ to 6 years, were on the floor with large sheets of paper and crayons with which they were making letters. One boy had been taught quite a few of them. The others looked up to him and seemed eager to copy his letters. After a bit, one of them said, "O is a good letter. O is a good letter." His mother who was watching the whole activity asked why.

"Because it's all there," he answered quickly. Could it be that the completeness of the circle, even the symbolism of a circle, has some meaning for a young child? Another boy said, "X is a bad letter. Something bad always happens wherever there is an X, like a train busting a car all up, or killing a bunch of guys."

Does the child of today feel connotations for certain letters which the child of yesterday did not have? One cannot lightly minimize the place letters occupy, even though we teach reading more by having the child get the picture of a word, phrase, or sentence as a whole rather than by learning the separate component parts. Ultimately, the component parts are learned, but the time for this varies so that some children miss it entirely because it wasn't done in this grade or that, the teacher in one grade taking it for granted that it was done in a previous grade. This uncertainty and variety of *what* to teach *when* is undoubtedly one reason so many children reach high school "not even knowing the alphabet."

Suppose, then, that the majority of children come to school possessing past experience with letters chiefly of the simple, basic letter shape. Actually, this situation is quite generally prevalent in the United States. Might it not be more truly a process of continuous learning if the first letters presented to them to read were the same as those letters with which they already were familiar? There are a few simple books using type like this. Some teachers who are using them find that children get the words much more quickly than they do in those printed more elaborately in Century or Gothic or Baskerville type faces, all commonly used in books today. Even as we have come to teach manuscript writing before cursive, we may come to realize that plain, basically shaped letters are a good first experience; these can be followed by the use of other types later on. There is room for much wider experimentation with books printed in this type and further study of their possible implications and advantages.

Following are a few books, set in this kind of type, which first and second grade teachers may find useful:

The Noisy Book	Margaret W. Brown	Harper
The Country Noisy Book		Harper
Two Little Trains		Scott
The Flower	Mary Louise Downer	Scott
The School Bus Picnic	Aaron Fine	Holt
Mystery of the Broken Bridge	Margaret Friskey	Children's Press
One Horse Farm	Dahlov Ipcar	Doubleday
Smart Mr. Tim	Helen Jarratt	Abingdon
Stick in the Mud	Jean and Fred Ketchum	Scott
True Book of Plants	John Lewellen	Children's Press
How Do You Travel?	Miriam Schlein	Abingdon
Little Red Nose		Abelard

The Sun Looks Down		Scott
All about Dogs,		Scott
Dogs, Dogs	Grace Skaar	
Nothing but Cats,		
Cats, Cats		Scott
The Very Little Dog		Scott
The Little Red House		Scott
This Is the Way the		
Animals Walk	Louise Woodcock	Scott

Most schools now teach children to write in manuscript, a form of writing which is easier for the large muscle adjustment of most six-year-olds, during first and second grades, changing to cursive writing at the end of second or the beginning of third grade.

Children like to read what they have written themselves. They like it so much that they read it over and over with genuine pride and satisfaction. Therefore, it is very likely they will enjoy at the time they are writing in this way the opportunity to read other people's stories printed in a book in just the same manuscript writing which they use for their own stories. Reports from use of these books in many first and second grades are very favorable. Here are a few books, printed in manuscript writing, which children enjoy for content, too:

Brownies Hush!	Gladys Adshead	Oxford
Tim Tadpole	Marjorie Flack	Doubleday
Millions of Cats	Wanda Gag	Coward
Everybody Has a House	Mary Green	Scott
The Bear Twins	Inez Hogan	Dutton
Plink, Plink	Leonard Kessler	Doubleday
Crunch, Crunch		Doubleday
Baby Bear	Hamilton Williamson	Doubleday
Lion Cub		Doubleday
Little Elephant		Doubleday
Monkey Tail		Doubleday

Because most children learn to read with basal series of readers which use some form of Century or Gothic type, it is advisable to have books which are printed in the same type. If some of these can be in large 24-point type, such as is used in a preprimer and primer, that is good. Others, set in 18-point type such as is used in most first and second grade readers, are good. These books are set in 24-point type:

Turtles	Wilfrid Bronson	Harcourt, Brace
Runaway Puppy	Margaret and Helen Johnson	Harcourt, Brace
Story of Rickey		Harcourt, Brace
Smallest Puppy		Harcourt, Brace

These are set in 18-point type:

Country Garage	Jerrold Beim	Morrow
Kid Brother		Morrow
Smallest Boy in Class		Morrow
Country	Margaret Buck	Abingdon
True Book of		
Air around Us	Margaret Friskey	Children's Press
The Lunch Box Story	Martha Goldberg	Holiday
The Green Thumb Story		Holiday
Sphinx	Robert McClung	Morrow
Tools for Andy	James S. Tippett	Abingdon
Search for Sammie		Abingdon

The placing of each phrase on one line makes Margaret Friskey's book easier to read, according to reports from many users. Helen Gentry, one of America's finest book designers, cautions against the use of too large type or too long lines of big type, since tests indicate that in some books the large type extends outside the child's normal eye span.

The Important Book by Margaret Wise Brown and illustrated by Leonard Weisgard is truly a most important book in every first and second grade. It presents many familiar phenomema in a child's experience—apples, spoons, grass, leaves, snow, clouds—and tells the most important characteristic or quality of each. It is excellent for starting conversation and discussion, but that is not its most important value. A different kind of type is used for each item. It is a good book for showing children the many kinds of type, the many slightly different ways of making the same letter while always keeping its basic shape. It is beautifully done and invaluable. At the end, the important thing about you is that "You are you"; this is presented in cursive writing. It is easy to see how helpful this can be when getting ready for that "important" transition from manuscript writing to cursive, also for that "important" wider use of many kinds of books printed in various ways.

Now comes the very weighty matter of content of the books capable of interesting beginning readers. Dick worried about "Oh, Oh" books being "dumb" when he came to read them on his own. Douglas considered those first offered to him such a bore that he would not even try to learn the words. Joan said, "They all run, run, run, but they never get anywhere. Who wants to read a story when nothing ever happens!"

You may say that it is only a few bright children who say things like these. *Not so few,* if we believe actual reports from widely separated places. Children of six and seven like action. They like things that go and they like the characters and animals in their stories to do something. If there is satisfying action, they quickly tell you that they like a book: "This is a good story," "This is a really interesting story." The content ought to be lively, to have action, to be interesting to the six- and seven-year-old. In order to be interesting, it should not be too far removed from his actual or possible experience. City children in the first or second grade may not like farm stories about cows and pigs which they have never seen.

This does not mean that all stories must be about the here-and-now. Children have imagination. Many very young children like imaginative stories. But the stories they read themselves are more likely to be here-and-now stories. The stories to be read to them can go further afield in ideas and concepts, both real and imaginary. A tale with folk flavor, like *Millions of Cats,* is a choice combination of realism and imagination.

The fantasy in the French elephant *Babar* has a strong appeal to many children.

There are a few exceedingly valuable books which truly give children concepts. In the book *All Falling Down* by Zion, everything does fall down—rain, apples, leaves, children. No first learning is necessary to recognize the words "fall down" here. The child wants to know the words because he wants to find out what happens.

This fact is also true of *Run, Run, Run* by Clement Hurd. When the dog jumps out to chase that cat and everything starts running in that exciting race, *run* takes on much more meaning than the isolated letters *r-u-n*. They all run, much happens, and they get somewhere.

Margaret Wise Brown's *Two Little Trains* is a most unusual story of two little trains going West:

> One little train was a streamlined train,
> Puff, Puff, Puff, going West.
> The other little train was a little old train,
> Chug, Chug, Chug, going West.

Here are two, different, interesting trains going somewhere. Then:

> Look down, look down
> That long steel track
> That long steel track
> Going West.

They come to a hill and get through it by going through a tunnel, and then:

> Look through
> Look through
> That long dark hill
> That long dark hill to the West.

So one goes clear to the "edge of the West," with the outside movement of the trains with their passengers and the inside concept of the track, tunnel, bridge and other things encountered on the journey. The external experience of the trains moving is illustrated in bold, bright colored pictures by Jean Charlot. The alternate pages are in black and white. They show "trackness," "tunnelness," "wetness," the inside concepts. A child once brought the book to his mother asking, "Please read me the train story where I go West that tells me how I feel inside as I go."

Another unusual book of this type, *Fast is not a Ladybug* by Miriam Schlein, is about the concepts of "fast" and "slow." It begins:

> Fast is not a ladybug crawling on a leaf.
> That is slow.

It goes on presenting in brief text and exciting pictures "fast" things, then slow things. There is a slow story of planting a seed which grows into a plant which bears a rose. That is slow because growing is always slow. Then follow some comparisons of what is fast for you and slow for you, and how both are good —a wonderful way of developing understanding of these concepts out of the child's knowledge of himself and his own experience.

Miss Schlein does a similar thing in helping a child get the concept of weight in her book, *Heavy is a Hippopotamus*, again by discussing familiar things—despite the title they really are familiar—and how ways of measuring weight have been developed in terms of the needs of each one of us. She does it for time in *It's About Time*.

All Kinds of Time is a small book about the concept of time by the poet Harry Behn. It is not really poetry, but it is poetic prose that evokes all sorts of thinking and realizing what time is. It is illustrated by the author with bright-colored, stylized pictures and sketches that pull the reader right along with the text. It stimulates much discussion and, frequently, much drawing. The realistic approach? The poetic approach? Both!

There are many easy-to-read stories which children really like, printed in 18- and 24-point type. Here are a few which are lively and of real interest to most children. They are stories of typical children, at home and at school, and of animals. In them, something *happens!*

Billy and Blaze (and others)	C. W. Anderson	Macmillan
Andy and the School Bus	Jerrold Beim	Morrow
Country Fireman		Morrow
Country Garage		Morrow
Kid Brother		Morrow
Smallest Boy in Class		Morrow
Tim and the Tool Chest		Morrow
Twelve O'Clock Whistle		Morrow
Two Is a Team (and others)		Harcourt, Brace
Little Old Truck	Jay Hyde Barnum	Morrow
The New Fire Engine		Morrow
Little Cowboy	Margaret Wise Brown	Scott
Little Fireman		Scott
Willie's Adventures		Scott
Sneakers		Scott
The Country Store	Margaret W. Buck	Abingdon
Lance's First Horse	Carolyn Coggins and Jack Holt	Whittlesey House
Flip	Wesley Dennis	Viking
Flip and the Morning		Viking
The Green Thumb Story	Jean Fiedler	Holiday
The School Bus Picnic	Aaron Fine	Holt
Angus and the Ducks	Marjorie Flack	Doubleday
The Story of Ping		Viking
Mystery of the Broken Bridge	Margaret Friskey	Children's Press
Trip for Johnny		Children's Press
Perking Little Engine		Children's Press
The Lunch Box Story	Martha Goldberg	Holiday
The Twirly Skirt		Holiday
Wait for the Rain		Holiday
Lost and Found	Kathryn Hitte	Abingdon
Letter for Cathy		Abingdon
Twin Colts (and others)	Inez Hogan	Dutton

Nappy Has a New Friend (and others)		Dutton
One Horse Farm	Dahlov Ipcar	Doubleday
Runaway Puppy	Margaret Johnson	Harcourt, Brace
Smallest Puppy		Harcourt, Brace
Story of Ricky		Harcourt, Brace
Plink, Plink	Leonard Kessler	Doubleday
Crunch, Crunch		Doubleday
The Happy Day	Ruth Krauss	Harper
Cowboy Small	Lois Lenski	Oxford
Little Farm		Oxford
Little Fire Engine		Oxford
Little Train		Oxford
Sphinx (a caterpillar)	Robert McClung	Morrow
Spike (a white-tail deer)		Morrow
Stripe (a chipmunk) and others		Morrow
One Is the Engine	Esther Meeks	Follett
The Elephant Herd	Miriam Schlein	Scott
Go with the Sun		Scott
When Will the World Be Mine?		Scott
How Do You Travel?		Abingdon
The Wet World	Norma Simon	Lippincott
The Very Little Dog	Grace Skaar	Scott
The Little Red House		Scott
Giddy-Ap	Charlotte Steiner	Doubleday
Pete's Puppets		Doubleday
Polka Dot (and others)		Doubleday
Tools for Andy	James S. Tippett	Abingdon
Search for Sammy		Abingdon
Follow the Road	Alvin S. Tresselt	Lothrop, Lee & Shepard
Follow the Wind		Lothrop, Lee & Shepard
Johnny Maple Leaf		Lothrop, Lee & Shepard
Rain Drop Splash!		Lothrop, Lee & Shepard

The humor of this age is rather slapstick; the behavior is rough and tumble; appearance is of minor importance, especially for boys. All these characteristics are reflected in the books they like best. Toward the end of third grade, a great interest in riddles becomes common—an interesting mixture of their particular sense of humor and genuine curiosity. A good riddle book will hold attention a long time, and it also gives a good opportunity for reading aloud.

Reading aloud for the purpose of revealing what a child does *not* know, thus lessening his self respect among his peers, is inexcusable. There should always be some legitimate reason for reading aloud, e.g., reading a riddle, the definition of a word from the dictionary, a funny story found in the paper or somewhere else, the label under a picture of something of interest to the group.

Since so many children are devoted to comics, it is an excellent idea to let them develop a comic strip around the current main interest or study. A strip of four or five pictures in simple stick drawing is easy to do. Children love to put the conversation into those balloons and to read it. As Joel said, "I like comics. You can always tell who says what."

Jerry welcomed a visitor to his room, a first grade, where a post-office unit was in full swing. They built a post-office, brought stamps, wrote letters and were deeply interested in anything that had to do with mailing letters and packages. As the visitor came in, Jerry said, "Would you like to hear the joke on me? It's in our comic today. The comic is about me and Miss S."

"Go ahead, Jerry," his teacher said. He giggled and so did the other children.

"Well," he began, "Miss S. writes lots of letters every Sunday. If she gets up in time Monday morning, she mails them on the way to school. If she gets up late, she has to hurry to get to school on time and doesn't have time to mail her letters. That's how it is most of the time. Then big kids like me who know

how to cross the street with care—you know, look both ways—
may mail her letters at recess or noon. So, yesterday morning,
I looked at this letter on her desk and asked her, 'Miss S., may
I mail that letter for you?'

"She said, 'Jerry, did you look at that letter carefully?'

"So I went over and picked it up to look at it, and the stamp
on it was pre-cancelled. Everyone laughed. Want to see the
comic?"

The visitor walked over. There it was in five pictures: Jerry
discovering the letter on the teacher's desk, Jerry asking Miss
S. whether he might mail it, Miss S. telling him to look more
closely, Jerry saying, "Oh, the stamp is pre-cancelled!" all the
children laughing, "Ha! Ha! Ha!" And they read "pre-cancelled
stamp" as well as "Ha!" Teachers who develop comic strips like
this with their children report amazing progress in reading improvement and spelling. One teacher in a fourth grade said,
"I'll never make a spelling list on the board again. I put them all
in balloons in our comics. It works!"

Picture dictionaries, both those made by children themselves
and simple ones, such as Oftedal's *My First Picture Dictionary*,
McBean's *Child's Picture Dictionary* and the *Golden Dictionary*, stimulate children's interest in words and in getting
acquainted with enough words to enable them to "read real
stories," as they often say. Children generally define a word in
terms of function: "A chair is to sit on," "A mother is to help
you."

Ruth Krauss has done a delightfully humorous word book, *A
Hole is to Dig*, which may stimulate much talk about words and
meanings. It is so much fun that children enter into the experience with it as though it were a game; they often want to
make their own word books. Most primary teachers use experience charts from which children enjoy reading the personal
experiences which they have narrated. Wider use of these
charts with books about the same things—dog, boy, girl, auto,
gas, service station, garage, train, fire engine—can well be made

by many teachers. The child who reads his own experience from a chart and a similar experience in a book is likely to think of reading as fun and more fun.

Many teachers label things in the room: chair, desk, table, children's names on chairs and lockers. Some people feel this does not really help children, since there is no special interest appeal. Additional labels which arouse interest are these:

Drawer for Secrets
Drawer for Surprises
Drawer for Good Ideas
Things to Use:
    Crayon
    Chalk
    Large paper
    Paste, etc.
Things We Need
Science Corner
Book Reading Corner
Music Corner
Our Museum
Bulletin board headings:
    Weather Today
    News from Our Families
    Cartoons
    Jokes
    Our Next Trip

The better the communication in any classroom or home among the children themselves, teachers and parents, parents and children, the more likely it is that reading will become easy for children. The better the rapport, the more ways in which reading is fun and a natural way to extend experience, the more likely is the pattern to be one of continuous learning. Then, reading becomes naturally and easily a handle to the reality of living.

A few specific books for beginning readers in the primary grades have been mentioned in this section because there is such a need to know these books—both their content and their format as designed to meet the special needs of young children.

A fuller discussion of books will follow in Chapters 5, 6, and 7. As children grow and enter the middle grades, there are marked changes in their growth pattern, characteristics, needs and interests.

These children, aged nine, ten and eleven years, begin to be interested in a group or a gang. They enjoy belonging to Cub Scouts, Brownie Scouts, a football or baseball team, Campfire Girls, a children's theater group. They still do not pay much attention to appearance because they are much more interested in the activity itself. It is a time of great physical vigor, of deriving great satisfaction from many strenuous physical activities. Games begin to have strong appeal, and the attention span is markedly longer. The ability to plan and to work for desired goals increases markedly.

In fourth and fifth grade, boys and girls work and play together happily with little concern about sex, except as it concerns prowess or strength. In sixth grade, a differentiation of interests often shows up. Girls are more mature than boys at this age and begin to show some of the characteristics of early adolescence. They giggle a lot. Some of them begin to be much interested in appearance and to seek attention from boys. Few boys of this age care anything about appearance and seldom show any interest in girls. Physically this is a period of rapid growth in bone structure. Girls often reach their full height by the age of twelve. All this lengthening out means awkwardness, clumsiness, even broken limbs. It is a time of gauche behavior, but also of tremendous increase in intellectual curiosity.

Many people are of the opinion that the heaviest reading period in life is that between the ages of ten and twelve. The mass media competes for time; so do clubs and other outside activities such as music, dancing, and sports. Many parents, especially those in the upper income brackets, want to give their children every possible advantage by providing many outside lessons at this time. Despite all this competition for his time and attention and many other pressures, the child who discovers what books can mean in his life reads profusely, especially if all kinds of books are easily accessible. He likes swift action in his books. He begins to want a good plot, a mystery, a problem to be solved. The episodic adventures of children and animals which have satisfied the child in primary grades are no longer adequate. There must be a good plot in any story that really becomes popular with this age group.

Charles was a third grader who came in for a browsing period at a book exhibit with the children of his room. He asked the person in charge of the exhibit, "May I look at those books over there?" pointing to a table of books for children in the upper grades.

"Yes, of course, if you want to," she replied.

"My teacher said I couldn't. She thinks I can't read them, but I can. She don't know that. You see, I don't like baby books. I like a book where something happens to the guy and he gets in trouble or something and it all has to work out." Charles struggled to define a plot.

"Oh, of course, I can't read every word on every page. But when I get to the bottom of a page and can hardly wait to turn it, I know what it's all about. But she don't know that."

His friend smiled. Thus encouraged, Charles looked up and asked, "Want me to tell you a secret? The more you read, the fewer words you have to skip. But she don't know that."

One hopes, however, that most teachers do know that "the more you read, the better you read, so the more you read." The child who is really able to read anything that interests him is mature enough to want a good plot and good characterization. He is interested in animals, especially horses. In this air age, a good horse story is tops in popularity! Dogs and wild animals follow along, but the story always must have action and adventure. He is interested in real people. The characters in a good story must be characters with whom he can identify himself, or the kind of people that he likes; they must be plausible, real people. He also develops a great interest in people who have

It is good to have plenty of books easily accessible.

We like to choose our own books.

Stratford Jr. High School, Arlington, Va.

We read a lot.

There are interesting problems to solve.

Dorcas Rosenfeld, South San Francisco Unified School Dist., Calif.

really lived and done interesting things; an interest in biography begins to develop. He is at an age of wanting to get facts, so information books and science books are in great demand. If these are functional in approach, suggesting experiments and things he can do in order to "find out," they are especially popular. If his creativity is stimulated by a lively schoolroom and home environment, he is much interested in books about hobbies, in books which tell how to make things like puppets or how to work with wood, clay, or leather.

There is likely to be a strong interest in series, through which one follows a beloved heroine like Laura Ingalls or Betsy Tacy or Alec and his black stallion on and on in his or her adventures. Perhaps this happens most often when a real identification takes place. Series are likely to develop in a period of insecurity such as a war or post-war era like the present one because they offer security. The child likes this book, this hero, this character. Knowing more about the character tends to build a child's faith that life does go on; thus it helps to establish a feeling of security. "More of the same" in an era of rapid change tends to help satisfy the need for reassurance. The great increase in series in these post-war years is an indication of this tendency.

The interest in heroes which often develops during these years, plus a sense of humor and a joy in the improbable or impossible, combine to give tall tales great appeal for this age. Children like the rare mixture of realism and utter impossibility in the tales of Pecos Bill, Paul Bunyan, Mike Fink, Old Stormalong, and Tony Beaver. The hero of an American tall tale is always a giant reflecting the American feeling that he is bigger and better or even biggest and best, an attitude characteristic of a younger, growing nation like ours.

The child of this age is apt not to like a book which is outsize because he thinks it may be a "baby book." He wants a real story in a book six by eight to eight and a half inches, and fairly thick, a typical novel size for his age. He likes the printed page not too crowded. The type should not be too small, the line not too long across the page. Double spacing helps. Many children look for quotation marks: "A book with plenty of talk is usually better" or "It is more lively." They also often say that they do not like "I" books—books told in the first person. Somehow they feel that there is usually not as much action in a first person narrative. Most children of this age still want illustrations in their books. A good picture on the jacket, a few full-page illustrations, or, at least, sketches at the beginnings of chapters definitely add to the appeal of a book for nine- to twelve-year-olds.

It is reassuring to know that there are many books to satisfy the needs and interests of all types of children aged nine, ten, and eleven years. In observing growth, it is evident that the growth pattern does not always follow a steadily mounting line; it is much more likely to go up in a stairlike pattern. The children seem to go along on a level for a while, then make a small or large spurt upwards, then follow the new level. Big spurts seem especially characteristic of seven-year-olds and twelve-year-olds. The seven-year-old is a child, not a baby; the twelve-year-old is an adolescent, not a child.

Probably adolescence brings the greatest number of changes, both physical and psychological, of any period in a child's growth. There are great modifications in characteristics, needs, and interests. The many physical changes tend to make young people restless, disturbed, uncertain, self-conscious. Certain traits such as shyness or aggressiveness may become greatly over-emphasized at this time. Growth patterns and growth rates vary widely, as does the change in different aspects of each individual's personality.

Most girls have nearly achieved their full growth in early adolescence; few of them increase in height after the ages of twelve, thirteen, or fourteen. For most of them, the period following this is one of slowing down in growth. For boys, on the other hand, this is usually a time of rapid growth. They spurt ahead, developing faster than girls of the same age and attaining intellectual and physical maturity.

Most girls become interested in boys at this age. They giggle a lot and do many things to attract attention. They are greatly interested in their appearance and think nothing of taking an hour or two to dress and get "made up" for a date. Some boys become interested in girls, more often at fourteen and later than at twelve and thirteen. They, also, then pay more attention to "looks," slicking their hair down and even cleaning fingernails. Here, again, television and movies reveal so much adult experience that in many areas those age levels are getting lower. It was a ten-year-old who recently said, "Haven't you got a really good book that tells you how to get along with girls? All the kids in my room (fifth grade) take girls to the movies on Saturday. I ask a girl on Thursday or Friday and she says yes. Then she always calls me up Friday night and says no. I don't know what the trouble is, but I'll tell you it ain't B.O.!" He was beginning early!

Many studies of child development and adolescence give far more detailed analysis than is justified in this book. Both teachers and parents should read several of these books and monographs in order to be prepared to understand all the characteristic changes of this period.

Certain behavior problems and attitudes toward discipline typical of the twentieth century adolescent were not characteristic of an adolescent one or two generations ago. We are moving out of an authoritarian era in most aspects of our social order. The belief that discipline should come from within, not from without, is more and more widely accepted. This is more true in America than in any other place in the world. Many feel that American children are spoiled. Be that as it may, self discipline is probably the highest form of regulation when it is sincere. If it results only in selfishness—getting one's own way and having no respect for others—it is poor discipline or a lack thereof. This fact explains why some of "those big boys" are very difficult to handle. To understand how our social order, most of our family training, "child-centered" schools, and other organizations such as clubs and camps all tend to follow newer ways of discipline will help in understanding the young people themselves. As one realizes they are the product of these training methods, one may be more patient with difficult behavior and more willing to guide individuals toward attitudes which work for the good of the whole group.

Group loyalties are very strong at this time. Sports are a dominant interest, so the team is very important. Teamwork has real meaning when it is closely related to a child's success or failure. Adolescents, loyal to their own peer group, do not want to look or be different. If a crew cut is popular, every boy wants his hair cut so. If it is "the thing" to wear an oversize shirt hanging outside the belt, every girl wears it so. They all use the same slang, the same double talk. Nothing dates one so quickly as familiarity with current words and their special meanings. The same dance, the same popular music, the same sports hero, the same movie or television star is accepted by all the bobby-soxers —all the gang. These loyalties are strong and may supersede loyalty to the family and home for a time.

Both boys and girls feel quite grown-up and want adult privileges. They feel that they "know" far more than their parents and are quite ready to tell their parents what life is all about. Actually many of them do know more than some parents; they now know more than ever before in their lives. Their thinking begins to move into the realm of ideas. History becomes not so much a study of men and events as of concepts such as freedom, the democratic way of life, civic responsibility, international interdependence, world trade, human relations, cooperation and brotherhood. Many young people reason and think well when they are stimulated to probe beneath the surface of events; they try to understand how and why life is as it is.

Education used to be primarily concerned with training the mind. Gradually, some concern with training the body developed. Now, education is concerned with developing the *whole* child. Only when there is concern for the spirit, too, can education be adequate for life. Our kind of scientific era stresses the great need for knowledge, for knowing the facts. If education is concerned with developing the whole child, however, it is just as important that the child should feel in his experience the impact of beauty and goodness. Books can meet all these needs and interests—spiritual, physical, and intellectual.

It is inevitable that some separation of interests should evolve at this age level. Boys are greatly interested in science fiction, sports, high adventure at sea, mountain climbing or exploring, great people, successful people, and history when told with enough exciting adventure. They read no so-called "girls' books." Girls read all boys' books as well as girls'. Most of them read more than boys at this age. They begin to want an element of romance in their fiction and they often become rather sentimental and hero-worshipping. This adoration of older women who have done interesting things often gives a basis for directing a girl's interests. That excellent story of Florence Nightingale, *Lonely Crusader*, appeals to many girls who think they want to be nurses. *In the Big Time*, an excellent account of successful people in the entertainment world with plenty of emphasis upon the hard work involved in really making the "big time," is good for the stage-struck girl who wants to go to Hollywood.

Warm human biographies of great and good and successful people can reveal much to young people, both ideas and ideals, and can help them gain a sense of direction in their own lives. Future education, life work, and careers are a large concern of the child entering high school; all during this period, career stories are of vital interest. These career stories should be written well enough to stand on their own characterization, not just superficial, written-to-order yarns about some career likely to appeal to a girl, such as fashion designing or being an airplane stewardess or high-powered saleswoman. Too often, such stories are presented with emphasis on the glamour rather than the nature of the work. A career story should stem from knowledge of the work, should evolve from the actual human value of the characters.

Many parents and teachers are baffled by the boy who does not want to read, who is interested only in sports. Maybe such a boy will read the life stories of Jim Thorpe, Lou Gehrig, or Christy Matthewson. From such vital accounts of people with interests like his own, he may soon go on to biographies of other great or successful people in science or world affairs, such as Albert Einstein, Albert Schweitzer, Ralph J. Bunche, or Trygvie Lie. Sometimes, young people who have not had happy experience with poetry think that it is sissy. Good narrative poetry like that of Benet or Masefield or Noyes is very interesting. When a ballad such as "On Top of Old Smoky" becomes a popular song and ballad singers like Burl Ives become popular, an interest in ballads and the stories they tell may develop like wildfire.

Adolescents are quick to take up any "rage," and one can build worthwhile projects from their fads and foibles by going along with them. In this age of realism, they frankly say of the sports hero who always wins, of the love story that always ends happily, "But that's not how it is in real life; we'll take it *straight*." In this age of speed, they are very time conscious. There isn't time to read much, so the book must not be too long. If a story, it must move swiftly; they have little patience with lengthy explanations or long descriptions. They constantly ask for "thin books for which you can get credit."

Type should not be too small, nor the page too crowded. Double spacing, easier to read, makes a strong appeal. If a book is easy to read because of its physical format and appearance, it will be much more widely read. It may be full of ideas, but not moralistic. It may present plenty of problems, but answers and results are not necessary. It may discuss all aspects of love and human relations, but a happy ending is not necessary. Just because adolescence is a period of such conflict, such swift and sudden change in interest and behavior, it demands resources covering a wide range of interest. Its very exaggerations may mean a wacky sense of humor, but also greater sensitivity to beauty; irritating cocksureness, but also genuine concern for facts; casual behavior, but also eager pursuit of knowledge of the world and of man. The world is their oyster; they are cracking it wide open in their own way.

Despite all the democratic ideals of America, the Christian ideals of peace and brotherhood of man, and concern for the four freedoms, this twentieth century world which we are handing on to them is not a very good world. There are more instruments of destruction than in all history; more strife, conflict, ill will, hot wars, cold wars; greater lack of agreement and failure to solve problems through reasonable arbitration; less cooperation than in all history. Is it any wonder that the adolescent is bewildered? Why is our world so far from achieving its ideals?

This is a time for long, long thoughts. As we think of all the possible ways in which we can help growing children and young people to see and hold on to that which is good, the resource offered by good books is one to take advantage of. To use it, they must like to read. If the reading experience is easy, happy, and satisfying, the chances for knowing both what is good and what is important in your own life are greater. Generally speaking, the reading child is better equipped to meet his world.

These are a few of the goals for which many kinds of books may prove of value to a maturing young person:

1. There should be a steady expansion of concepts about man and his world.

2. There should be a vital extension of experience that goes beyond the limits of time and space—backward or ahead in time and across, through, or beyond any place or space of the universe.

3. There should be a persisting, increasing clarification of ideas, based on knowledge and leading toward a truer sense of relationships.

4. There should be deepening of conviction as experience, knowledge, and ideologies become a part of our intellectual activity.

5. There should be heightening of awareness, with increasing response to all sensation, all possible experience.

6. There should be genuine development of critical thinking with sincere objectivity and increase in ability to observe and evaluate.

All of these goals should stimulate individual creativity, increasing self-expression and usefulness to the whole social order. It is evident, therefore, that it is important for teachers and parents to know books which may be a rich resource for such living and learning and to have them available. The following three chapters discuss some of the books which help to achieve such goals, books which are not time-fillers or time-killers, but actual resources which may meet growing children's needs and interests. Books do not hold all the answers, but they do point the way and equip the traveler for the journey; they open his eyes that he may see, open his ears that he may hear, free his spirit that he may soar. There is walking, there is running, there is riding, and there is soaring for the human mind and spirit.

5

Books to Help Children Understand and Adjust to the Physical World

*P*ROBABLY the child's first basic need for developing a sense of security is that of understanding the physical world about him. It is frequently taken for granted that he does know the physical world in which he lives. However, living in this house, playing in this yard, walking down this street to this school day after day after day does not necessarily mean that a child feels at home in that familiar physical environment. He may, and he may not. Familiarity is not enough; it is not *knowledge*.

It is interesting to discover in several recent studies of emotionally disturbed and maladjusted children how large a percentage of their difficulties began in the physical realm. Children in the primary grades ask a staggering number of questions, not just to get attention as is so often true of the three-year-old, but to learn about this physical world: Where did I come from? What makes me grow? What makes animals and trees grow? What makes a train go? How can an airplane fly? Books can extend first hand experience by sharing information and knowledge that is satisfying to the six-, seven-, and eight-year-old. Therefore, this interest is often one of the strongest ones with which to help a child discover how much reading can mean. Books answer many spontaneous questions and satisfy many needs to know. They also enrich the content of text and reference books by giving the child an opportunity to read in detail about some subject only briefly discussed in a textbook.

Tommy was nearly ten years old and in third grade, having repeated first and second grades. He was a non-reader, an unhappy child in school, and a discipline problem. A special exhibit of books was brought to his school one day. He wandered around awhile, finally walking over to a table of easy science and nature books. He found one called *Starlings* by Wilfrid Bronson. Pretty soon he came up with eyes shining, fairly shouting.

"I just found out. I just found out! All my life I've been trying to find out. I asked my dad a thousand times and he don't know. I asked my teacher about a hundred times, and she don't even know where to find out.

"Why can birds stay up in the air and we can't? Why?

"Look, here it is. See this picture and these words? Birds have air pockets over their guts and we haven't. That's why! I found it out myself in a book. I can't read all the words yet, but I will."

And he did. Tommy was interested in flying more than anything else in this whole, wide world. First he read *Cloud Hoppers*. He called it a silly book, but explained he had to begin with an easy one. Then he read *The Little Airplane*, then *Airplane Andy*. But now, he was reading on his own. He wanted to know about so many things that he couldn't try hard enough to tackle any book which told him what he wanted to know. Soon he read far better than most children in his room. He is eleven years old now and in sixth grade, reading avidly, doing good work in arithmetic and social studies. Flying is still his "handle to reality." He knows more about it than many adults. His interest, his need to know, opened the door for him, as it can for other children.

Today's books about the physical world include many informative volumes, experimental books of tests for scientific principles, biographies of scientists, and what we call science fiction. The science fiction ranges from stories of a magnet or ranch or rain or animals to the space thrillers for teen-agers and adults. These books should meet the same high standards as are expected from any scientific material for adults. The information must be accurate in terms of what is known at the present time. The illustrations should be clear and accurate. All explanations, captions of pictures, and illustrations should be clear enough for children to read and understand. The material should be logically organized and well indexed. The content should challenge the child to seek further information, to observe carefully and widely, to question what he observes, to relate it to past experience, and to think for himself.

Of course, the author must be qualified to explain and interpret his subject. Actually, many scientists—first ranking men in their fields—are writing science books for children and young people today. These books are not written down to children, although the selection and presentation of the subject matter is appropriate for the age of the reader for whom the book is intended. It is interesting to note how many of these books are functional in approach, relating the subject being discussed or explained to the child and his living.

Books about the Physical World for Children to Age 8

Most six-, seven-, and eight-year-olds are greatly interested in themselves and where they came from, their own bodies and how they grow. This is natural, since much of their learning in the first six years of life has been through the senses.

What's Inside of Me? is a new kind of book by Zim. Herbert S. Zim is making one of the finest contributions to children's understanding of their physical world through his books and his teaching. This book is for a parent and child or teacher and small group to read together some simple but interesting facts about the human body. There are excellent pictures also. Every so often, there is a short section giving some especially interesting information in larger type for the child to read himself. It encourages a child to discover that he, himself, can read about something of real interest to him. Experience with the book shows that it affords many children deep satisfaction.

Egg to Chick, All About Eggs, and *All Kinds of Babies* all by Selsam, show how we get an egg from a chicken and a chicken from an egg and the different kinds of eggs in which new life starts. They give a simple introduction to the life cycle of animals and human beings. Hayne's *True Book of Health* is just right for a five- or six-year-old to find out about his body and how to keep it well. Pearl Buck tells of the beginning of life in story form in *Johnny Jack and His Beginnings.*

The next group of books tell the life story of different birds and animals, satisfying the desire to find out about growth and how living creatures live. The type is large, the pictures closely related to a child's experience, as in *Turtles* by Bronson, *Frogs and Toads* by Zim, *Sphinx* (a caterpillar) by McClung. Each of these authors has several more fine life cycle books about other living creatures. Because birds are a part of most younger children's experience, there are quite a few books about them:

Every Day Birds	Allen
Starlings	Bronson

Robins in the Garden	Earle
True Book of Birds We Know	Friskey
Birds at Home	Henry
Ruby Throat	McClung

These are not just descriptive books; they are functional. They take the child into real experience with birds in terms of his probable interests. A group of teachers in a summer workshop found fifteen common interests of third graders in the book *Starlings*, for example, flying, planes, wings, nests, what birds eat. This is the same book which was the "open sesame" for Tommy of the above story.

Zim's *What's Inside of Animals?* is similar to *What's Inside of Me?* and will probably satisfy the child who wants to know the inside as well as outside story of life.

Podendorf's *True Book of Animal Babies* describes animals that must be cared for while young.

All Around You by Bendick is a delightful, accurate introduction to what lives and grows in yards, fields, and other places to which most children have daily access. The sketches add greatly to its interest.

Harriet Huntington opens a child's world in four books with beautiful photographs:

Let's Go Outdoors
Let's Go to the Brook
Let's Go to the Desert
Let's Go to the Seashore

Children will look at these pictures over and over, and then go out to find the same thing. Or, they will find a caterpillar or turtle, then come in to find out about it in the book. The stimulation and satisfying answers to information desired indicate how beautifully the books work both ways.

This growing world includes flowers, all kinds of plants, and trees. Here, too, Zim's *What's Inside of Plants?* gives full information. An excellent beginning book with extra large type and clear, simple drawings, well arranged, is *The True Book of*

Plants We Know by Miner. *The True Book of Weeds and Wild-flowers* and *The True Book of Trees* by Podendorf are also satisfying. Selsam has an excellent group of books about how to grow many kinds of plants:

Play with Plants
Play with Leaves and Flowers
Play with Trees
Play with Vines

Webber has another group about how things grow. *Up Above and Down Below,* with interesting drawings and a brief text, shows what grows above the surface of the earth, what below. It is easy to see how storage roots like carrots, potatoes, and onions make good food, or how leafy green things like lettuce and cabbage make another kind of good food. In *Travelers All,* a child learns how many different kinds of seeds start new plants in other places. In *Anywhere in the World,* he learns about the effects of heat and cold, dryness and moisture upon all growing things, and he also discovers that man has learned to adapt himself to live anywhere in the world. *Bits that Grow Big* will start anyone growing many kinds of plants. *Thanks to Trees* not only tells how trees grow, but makes clear their uses and value to us. Gould's *Very First Garden* is just right for help in planting one's first garden.

A natural interest likely to evolve next is the earth below us and the stars above. Concern with the inanimate elements of our physical world naturally follows interest in living things; hence, our discussion is in the order of a child's probable sequence of interests.

Here, too, Zim can start us well with *What's Inside the Earth? What's in the Sky?* by Dunham and *You Among the Stars* by the Schneiders are good books with which to start knowing those heavens above. Lewellen's *True Book of Moon, Sun, and Stars* and Friskey's *True Book of the Air Around Us* are not only easy to read but satisfactory in content for beginning readers. In the *True Book of the Air Around Us* one concept is given on each line, just the way a child is helped to read more easily at this age. Here, content, format, and child interest meet perfectly.

The Schneiders also must become the special friends of all who know what it can mean to children to really know their physical world. Herman and Nina Schneider have a lively family of their own. After years of teaching in New York and Dr. Schneider's recent service as science coordinator for New York public schools, they are now devoting all of their time to writing science books for children. The large number of their satisfying books is steadily increasing. Notice how even the titles of the next three indicate a functional approach. These books explain good ways to learn about how things work:

Let's Find Out (questions concerning the science of chemistry)

Now Try This (questions concerning the science of physics)

Let's Look inside Your House (scientific explanations of common household things that work by electricity or other such means)

In Toys at Work, Lewellen introduces children to the underlying principles of physics through the use of these principles in common toys. We begin where we are, with the immediate experience which lays a sound foundation for comprehending the scientific principles later on. Such a functional approach in terms of a child's immediate experience has real meaning to the child.

There are a few stories based upon true life experience which are of great interest to children of this age:

All Ready for Winter by Adelson (how animals get ready for winter)

Restless Robin by Flack (bird migration)

Tim Tadpole by Flack (a tadpole grows into a frog)

Wait for the Rain by Goldberg (two boys and the rain)

The Big Snow by Hader (feeding birds and small animals after a big snowstorm)

Go with Sun by Schlein (how animals spend the winter)

Time for Sleep by Selsam (animal habits)

Billy Goes Exploring by Sterling (Billy discovering his nearby world, excellent photographs)

Sophie and Her Puppies by Sterling (a dachshund family, excellent photographs)

Baby Jack and Jumping Jack Rabbit by Tireman (true picture of desert life)

Follow the Wind by Tresselt (the story of wind)

Johnny Mapleleaf by Tresselt (a fall story)

Rain Drop Splash by Tresselt (story of water)

White Snow Bright Snow by Tresselt (story of snow)

The Storm Book by Zolotow (a reassuring story of the coming and going of a big storm)

Books for Children Age 9 to 11

Interest in the physical world becomes stronger and stronger as children grow. We live in a scientific age in which new discoveries constantly change the way we live—the automobile, the refrigerator, TV, vitamins, antibiotics, to name a few recent things important in today's ways of living. Children's interest is aroused in these things. The newspaper, radio, and television present discussion on all sorts of scientific discoveries and activities. Such scientific knowledge is not confined to the laboratory or the classroom. It affects the common things we do at home every day—what we eat, our health. It is part of common interest, common knowledge, not specialized knowledge for a classroom. Much of it is, and should be, specialized; much of what radio and television talk about as if it were scientific fact is only commercial advertising. All these elements combine to arouse strong child interest in the scientific world and, at the same time, to indicate the importance of seeing that the facts and information which children get are accurate facts, not merely commercial propaganda.

The nine-, ten-, or eleven-year-old is still much interested in himself. Baruch's *My Body and How it Works* is a good first book to read. The Schneider's *How Your Body Works* is really a functional physiology—not just a description of a skeleton, nerves, blood vessels, and muscles, but a lively presentation of children doing things they want to do, with interesting discussion of what the body must be like to do it well.

Clark came rushing into the school library one day. He was ten years old and in fifth grade. He did not read much. When he did, it was usually a mystery tale or a horse story.

"Got any books about health?" he asked.

"For yourself?"

"Uh-huh. I want to play baseball and I'm no good. My muscle is soft as a tomato. Just feel it," he said, as he bent his elbow and presented his arm. "I'd like to find out whether it's because my mother doesn't feed us right or the fault of the coach," he continued with a serious look.

Can you imagine how much it meant to find *How Your Body Works* with a picture of a boy on the front throwing a baseball! Clark found that neither of his guesses was correct and learned a great deal about what his body needed in order that he might develop strong muscles for throwing or catching a ball.

For general exploration along nature's highway, there are many good books with attractive illustrations such as Buck's *In Woods and Fields* and *In Yards and Gardens*, Doane's *A Book of Nature*, Parker's large *Golden Book of Natural History*. Snakes, insects, ants, bees, all become very interesting to a young explorer of the natural world. Bronson's *Wonder World of Ants* gives a fascinating, accurate picture of the complex pattern of ant life. Zim's *Snakes*, Hoke's *First Book of Snakes*, Tibbett's *First Book of Bees*, Williams' *First Book of Bugs*, give the kind of accurate information anyone is likely to want when first interested in these living creatures. A good fourth grade reader can read most of the books in this excellent "First Book of" series, but the content and fine pictures will be of interest to everyone, including adults. Zim's *Goldfish* gives much general information about fish and specific information about keeping goldfish. For children who want to build a large aquarium with varieties of water life, Morgan's *Aquarium Book* is excellent.

Learning to identify birds by appearance or song, following their migrations, attracting them to feeding stations, knowing their nesting habits, and watching them train their young is a fascinating hobby to begin young and keep throughout life. It is a good hobby for a whole family to share, for it sets no age limits. Bird charts and records are interesting for anyone to keep. Peterson's *Junior Book of Birds,* Reed's *Bird Guide,* Zim's *Birds* are good identification books. Williamson's *First Book of Birds* is a good general discussion of bird structure and habits. Neurath's *Wonder World of Birds* is a good introduction. Webb's *Birds in their Homes* has interesting text and large colored pictures of several familiar birds and their nests, with special appeal for young children. Earle's *Birds and their Nests* is a smaller book with more detailed valuable information; her *Thunder Wings* tells the life story of a ruffed grouse. Zim also tells the life cycle of each type of bird in *Homing Pigeons and Owls. All About Birds* by Lemmon gives much satisfying information. Zim's *Elephants, Golden Hamsters,* and *Rabbits* give the life cycle of each of these animals. The books on hamsters and rabbits also give careful instructions on how to raise and care for them. Neurath's *Wonder World of Animals,* Schmidt's *Homes and Habits of Wild Animals,* Semrad's *The Zoo* are not just picture books, but good, general information books about many kinds of animals. Blough's *When You Go to the Zoo* explains life habits and care of zoo animals as a scientist would describe them.

In the "First Book of" series, Cormack's *First Book of Trees* is an excellent introductory book of familiar trees of the United States. McKenny's *Trees of the Countryside* has beautiful colored illustrations of well-known trees and is more appealing because of its beauty. The Buffs have told the life story of California's giant redwoods in *Big Tree.* The distinguished drawings make this a choice book to own.

As we develop more interests, we go from animate to in-animate things. Earth and water are important phenomena to know about if children are to understand their world. Meyer's *Picture Book of the Earth*, Cormack's *First Book of Stones*, Cavanna's *First Book of Sea Shells*, and Dudley's *Sea Shells* are good ones with which to begin. Evans' books, *Rocks* and *Shells*, each come with a small beginning collection of rocks and shells. The Fentons' *Land We Live On* has many possibilities for use other than just reading it for information. There are excellent photographs of buttes, mesas, gullies, valleys, and other land formations. The text describing them is brief rhythmic prose. Rhythmic prose describing formations made by centuries of rhythmic formation gives an interesting association. A fifth grade prepared a most interesting program based on this book. The boys made slides from the photographs. The girls in a choral speaking group chanted those rhythmic, factual descriptions with true feeling.

Norling's *First Book of Water* and Walsh's *Water, Water Everywhere* are interesting reading matter about the cycle of rain which falls, nourishes life in the ground, runs off in rills, creeks, rivers, lakes, oceans, and is absorbed upward again to form clouds. Lane's *All About the Sea* adds information about the fascinating kinds of life in the sea to information about water. Such reading stimulates experiments and much creative activity.

So, too, does a study of the sky with its stars, planets, and constellations. Children may begin learning their names by studying charts and the sky itself. Often a whole family becomes interested in observing, reading, and making maps of the heavens. Fenton's *Worlds in the Sky*, Meyer's *Picture Book of Astronomy*, Johnson's *Stars for Children*, Frost's *Let's Look at the Stars*, Goodwin's *Real Book of Stars*, White's *All About the Stars*, and Neel's *Stars by Clock and Fist* offer a wide variety of charts and interesting reading.

It is exciting to follow weather changes, perhaps even to

build a weather station of one's own. Here is a fine way to encourage a science-minded, non-reading child to read, since he needs instructions to build such a station. Zim's *Lightning and Thunder* and *The Sun* are fascinating, easy reading. Meyer's *Picture Book of Weather* has fine charts. Schneider's *Everyday Weather and How it Works,* Spilhaus' *Weathercraft,* and Tannehill's *All About the Weather* have instructions for building one's own weather station, as well as much good information about what causes weather changes.

A real interest in experiments that show how things work and in learning what chemistry and physics are all about develops naturally at this age, especially in boys. Beeler and Branley have a fine group of books with great appeal to boys: *Experiments in Science, Experiments with Electricity, Experiments in Chemistry, Experiments with Airplane Instruments,* and *Experiments in the Principles of Space Travel.* The First *Book of Science Experiments* by Wyler and Freeman's *Fun with Science* and *Fun with Chemistry* are simpler books but interesting and easy to follow. Meyer has a *Picture Book of Chemistry, Picture Book of Electricity,* and *Picture Book of Molecules and Atoms.* Neurath's *If You Could See Inside, I'll Show You How it Happens* are colorful explanations of interesting and puzzling phenomena. There are several good general introductory books, highly readable, about many aspects of science in our world, of which these five are among the best:

What Makes It Tick?	Britton
Understanding Science	Crouse
How Things Work	Peet
It's Fun to Know Why	Schwartz
Through the Magnifying Glass	Schwartz

No child filled with " 'satiable curtiosity" needs to go along without satisfying it, even if he wants to go back a million years or more. There is Andrews' *All About Dinosaurs;* this explorer can make them interested after all his amazing explorations in the Gobi desert and elsewhere. Knight's *Life Through the Ages* has excellent, large pictures with a brief text that will absorb any child with a similar interest. Dickinson's *First Book of Prehistoric Animals,* Bloch's *Dinosaurs,* Neurath's *Wonder World of Long Ago* are other interesting introductions to prehistoric times.

Zim has a group of small, colorful, authentic, identification books, small enough to fit in a pocket, informative enough to satisfy all but advanced students:

Birds
Flowers
Insects
Reptiles and Amphibians
Stars
Trees

There are also some true-to-life stories that will start science-minded children reading when nothing else will. Mary Adrian has four life cycle stories full of interesting details: *Gray Squirrel, Honey Bee, Garden Spider, Fiddler Crab.* Glenn Blough, formerly a science specialist in the United States Office of Education, knows how to inform children in his tree story, *Tree on the Road to Turntown;* his story of rain, *Not Only for Ducks;* his story of sunshine, *Wait for the Sunshine;* his conservation story, *Look Out for the Trees,* and a zoo as seen through the eyes of a scientist, *When You Go the Zoo.* Eberle's *Hop, Skip and Fly,* Marcher's *Monarch Butterfly,* Leyson's *Manty the Mantis,* Sears' *Downy Woodpecker, Tree Frog,* and *Barn Swallow* are similar life cycle stories. Striking photographs add greatly to the interest of Kane's *Wild Wood Tales* of a whitefoot mouse, a moth, and a crow. Dorothy Lathrop's beautiful drawings of little animals and appealing story in *Let Them Live* arouses children's concern for conservation of wild life.

Jane Tompkins' stories of pairs of wild animals are vivid and exciting: *The Snow Shoe Twins, The Raccoon Twins, The Beaver Twins,* and several more. Alice Gall and Fleming Crew surely know animal life and the out-of-doors. Their true-to-life stories of animals make fascinating reading: *Flat Tail,* a beaver, *Ring Tail,* a raccoon, *Wag Tail,* a frog, and *Winter Flight,* about bird migrations.

The Norling's Pogo stories are concerned with many real child interests. *Pogo's House* tells the story of lumber and *Pogo's Mining Trip* decribes the earth's treasures. Not only colorful full page pictures but explanatory marginal sketches and lively narrative tell the story of a tree on the Sante Fe trail in Holling C. Holling's *Tree in the Trail.* This is a book to look at again and again; it appeals to children of all ages, even if it takes a good reader to read it.

The Schneiders have an unusual, beautiful book, *Follow the Sunset,* which is hard to place in any category but is a wonderful book to live with. It begins with a picture of the globe high on a page where the sun is setting in the eastern part of the United States. Text and pictures show father's home-coming, the evening meal, getting ready for bed, mother's goodnight lullaby. As the earth turns, we follow the sunset to Mexico, to the West coast, to Pacific Islands and China, and on around the world. Clothes differ, the food is different, but everywhere at the sunset hour, families do the same things. Father comes home from work, mother gets the evening meal, and the family goes to bed. One learns about the revolving earth and about fascinating people who live in different parts of the earth: it is a book of information, understanding, and beauty.

Ned had just found out about the world being round and was completely fascinated by the fact that he could stick on to the earth while it revolved and that the Chinese boy opposite him could do likewise. He looked down at his feet and the earth a long time and then said, "Ain't it wonderful to live on the earth!"

And so it is, and to discover more and more about it through first-hand experience and books that illumine experience is exciting adventure for anyone.

Books for Children Age 12 and up

The many changes which adolescence brings make a full understanding of one's own body more essential than ever. Understanding of procreation is necessary, but should not come suddenly. The child who has grown up with *Egg to Chick, All About Eggs, Story of a Baby*, and life cycle books of animals has a natural understanding of bodily functioning. Reproduction so that life may continue on the earth is a natural process. Novikoff's *From Head to Foot* is an excellent book for adolescents to read after *How My Body Works*. It adds the reproductive system to the respiratory, digestive, circulatory, and eliminative systems. The presentation in terms of possible ways the person may think about himself and what makes him click, the colorful, cartoon-like but accurate drawings make the book truly fascinating reading. Follow this with Ravielli's *Wonders of the Human Body* and the child discovers not only how perfect a machine the body is, but also the spiritual gifts that set man above all other creatures.

Lewellen explains how the brain functions in *You and Your Amazing Mind*. The book is based upon some work which Mr. Lewellen did with Dr. Karl Menninger in preparing recordings for young people at Dr. Menninger's clinic. These four books ought to be around in school and at home where children and young people can return to them again and again as needed. Many teachers after reading them have said, "These explain our minds and bodies better than anything I have ever read. I have learned so many things I never learned in a college course in physiology. They are good for all of us. I would put them first in a *must have* list."

In *Your Blood and You*, Dr. Riedman gives additional valuable information for the person who wishes to know how blood nourishes the body, how the white corpuscles and red function, how the heart, veins, and arteries work, and how they can keep them at their best. This, too, is important basic knowledge.

Understanding human reproduction is quite different from knowledge of plant and animal reproduction. Sex information is not just the so-called "facts of life" or physical information. Doctors Levine and Seligman base their books about reproduction upon all of the physical and psychological factors involved in creating a human baby, stressing the fact that a human baby is born because two people love each other and wish to create a home in which a human being may live and grow happily. So, their books, A Baby Is Born and The Wonder of Life, are a new kind of "sex education" book, also good to have always easily available. Frances Strain has written a number of books helpful to adolescents in understanding themselves, including Being Born. Zim's Mice, Men and Elephants is really a mammology, but is an excellent basis for understanding the structure of all mammals including ourselves. Physiology, sex education, reproduction, and life cycle need not and should not be disparate sections of study and information; all should be parts of one, whole understanding of life. These books make possible such comprehension. No wonder the reading child has a greater chance of being an adjusted child!

The natural world around us is a treasure house of beauty, wide interests, variety of life. Comstock's Handbook of Nature Study is one of the fullest descriptive books of this natural world and an invaluable reference. Nisenson's Picture Book of Nature is a briefer collection of information about the natural world. Older children are ready to go beyond first observation of nature. It is interesting now to discover natural laws at work, patterns of life common to all living things. Andrew's Nature's Ways and Tabell's Nature Was First take one into this realm of understanding. Snakes Alive by Pope is an amazing book about snakes and how they live. Teale's Boy's Book of Insects, Lane's All About the Insect World, and Harpster's The Insect World open up all the intricacies of moth, butterfly, ant, and insect life.

Long ago, Fuertes did an exhaustive study of all the birds of

America with excellent color pictures. This is now available in Pearson's *Birds of America*. That amazing person, John James Audubon—naturalist, artist, wanderer—drew pictures of many, many birds which he saw as he wandered over America. These were first published as a set of plates, which have become of great value both as works of art and pictures of bird life. They are now available in several editions, at different prices, under the title *Audubon's Birds of America*.

Roger Tory Peterson's *Field Guide to Birds* is one of the most satisfying identification bird books. All children who love birds, who are bird watchers, who are members of the Audubon Society, will read all there is in bird books like these. At least one of them belongs in every home or school.

Boy Scouts often become much interested in identifying animal tracks and learning much about how animals really live. Mason's *Animal Tracks, Animal Homes, Animal Sounds,* and *Animal Weapons* have real lure for boys with this interest. Working for a scout badge in this area will start and keep a boy reading books like these. Hogner's *Animal Book* and *Farm Animal Book* contain excellent pictures and full information for older children sincerely interested in animals. Van Dersal's *Wild Life in America* is especially good wherever there is concern for preserving wild life. Conservation-minded young people will find this good reading.

How the earth assumed its present form is an inexhaustible interest which is likely to grow much stronger at this age. The Fentons take us far back in earth's beginnings in *Earth's Adventures* and *Life Long Ago*, as does Scheele in those handsomely illustrated large books, *Prehistoric Animals* and *The First Mammals*. The Fentons continue it to the present in *Rocks and Their Stories* and *Riches from the Earth*. The Schneiders add to this kind of knowledge in *Rocks, Rivers and the Changing Earth*, as do Reed's *Earth for Sam*, Wyler's *Planet Earth*, Zim's *Minerals*. Galt's *Volcano*, Coleman's *Volcanoes New and Old* and Pough's *All About Volcanoes and*

Earthquakes are wonderful pictures of these still-active cones changing the earth's surface. Van Dersal's *Land Renewed* stimulates interest in soil conservation today. Reed's *Sea for Sam*, Riedman's *Water for People*, and Lane's *All About the Sea* answer many questions about the place and function of water on this planet.

Interest in stars should never wane. Books to add to those mentioned above are Williams' *Dipperful of Stars*, Baker's *When the Stars Come Out*, Reed's *Stars for Sam*, and White's *All About the Stars*. Branley's book on *Mars* and Lewellen's *You and Space Neighbors* tie the interest in conquering space to an interest in the stars and planets.

Plant life on the earth is an interest to keep developing with books such as Zim's *Plants* and Wall's *Gifts from the Forest*. Three fascinating books about many kinds of trees—how they grow and their uses—are Lane's *Story of Trees*, Rogers' *First Book of Tree Identification*, and Sterling's *Trees and Their Uses*.

It is quite natural for all science-minded young people to want to experiment widely—to really discover the laws of light, sound, electricity, atomic energy and all areas of science. This surely is a time one reads to know, and there are excellent books with just that knowledge. To learn about light, read Bishop's *Stepping Stones to Light*. For sound, there are Baer's *Sound: An Experiment Book* and Geralton's *Story of Sound*. For electricity, Morgan's *First Electrical Book for Boys*, Yates' *A Boy and A Battery*, and Shippen's *Bright Design*, give the whole exciting story of electricity from early discoveries to the present. Bischoff's *Atoms at Work*, Lewellen's *You and Atomic Energy* (really easy to comprehend), Yates' *Atomic Experiments for Boys*, and Hyde's *Atoms Today and Tomorrow* explain atomic energy.

For further exploration, there are Bendick's *Electronics for Young People*, Ross' *Radar and Other Electronic Inventions*, Morgan's *First Chemistry Book for Boys and Girls*, Yates' *Boys'*

Book of Magnets, Yates' *A Boy and a Motor,* Schneider's *Everyday Machines and How They Work,* as well as *More Power to You.* Lynn Poole has one of the most successful and popular television programs on the air, the Johns Hopkins Science Review. In accordance with correspondence revealing strong interests, he has put some of his scientific information into the books *Today's Science and You* and *Science the Super Sleuth.* All of this material provides reading very close to the interests of many young people today. There are also many true-to-life stories, especially, exciting wild animal stories, written by authors from first-hand experience. Sally Carrigher's *One Day on Beetle Rock,* for example, is an exciting book of first-hand observation in the High Sierra Mountains; written for adults, it fascinates young people, too. These stories have the double appeal of exciting adventure and accurate facts about how animals live:

Quest of the Snow Leopard	Roy Chapman Andrews
One Day on Beetle Rock	Sally Carrigher
Monte (a bear)	George Franklin
Tricky (a red fox)	
Wild Animals of the Southwest	
Sheba	
Little Fox	Frances Frost
Masked Prowler: Story of a Raccoon	John and Jean George
Meph, the Pet Skunk	
Vulpes, the Red Fox	
Vison, the Mink	
Rufus (a red fox)	Dorothy Childs Hogner
Chip, the Dam Builder (a beaver)	Jim Kjelgard
Haunt Fox	
Kalak of the Ice (a polar bear)	
Lion Hound (a mountain lion and dog)	
Persimmon Jim, the Possum	George Lippincott
Long Horn, Leader of the Deer	
The Phantom Deer	
Striped Coat, the Skunk	
Wahoo Bobcat	
Ben: A Wild Rabbit	

Pirate of the North	Harold McCracken
The Great White Buffalo	
Sentinel on the Snow Peaks	
The Biggest Bear on Earth	
Wings in the Woods	Robert McClung

The books presented in this chapter do not constitute a complete bibliography of books on science and nature study for children; there are hundreds more. Those discussed are good to live with. They also introduce many of the outstanding scientists who are interpreting the physical world for children today. Such accurate knowledge of the physical world is important in the life of every growing child; books like these ought to be an essential part of the resources of all schools and homes. Living with these books may well provide a first step in helping a child achieve many of the goals discussed at the close of the last chapter. This is their world.

Following is a list of science books discussed in Chapter 5.

Book List for Children to Age 8

General Information

Everyday Birds	Gertrude Allen	Houghton Mifflin
All around You	Jeanne Bendick	Whittlesey House
Turtles	Wilfrid S. Bronson	Harcourt, Brace
Starlings		Harcourt, Brace
Johnny Jack and		
His Beginnings	Pearl Buck	John Day
What's in the Sky?	Miriam P. Dunham	Oxford
Robins in the Garden	Olive L. Earle	Morrow
True Book of		
Air around Us	Margaret Friskey	Children's Press
True Book of		
Birds We Know		Children's Press
Very First Garden	Dorothea Gould	Oxford
True Book of Health	Olive V. Haynes	Children's Press
Birds at Home	Marguerite Henry	Donohue
Let's Go Outdoors	Harriet Huntington	Doubleday
Let's Go to the Brook		Doubleday

Let's Go to the Desert		Doubleday
Let's Go to the Seashore		Doubleday
True Book of Toys at Work	John Lewellen	Children's Press
True Book of Sun, Moon and Stars		Children's Press
True Book of Plants We Know	Irene Miner	Children's Press
Ruby Throat: Life of a Humming Bird	Robert McClung	Morrow
Sphinx: One Year in the Life of a Sphinx Caterpillar		Morrow
Spike: The Story of a White Tail Deer		Morrow
Stripe: The Story of a Chipmunk		Morrow
Tiger: The Story of a Swallowtail Butterfly		Morrow
Bufo: The Story of a Toad		Morrow
Let's Find Out	Herman and Nina Schneider	Scott
Let's Look inside Your House		Scott
Now Try This		Scott
You among the Stars		Scott
All about Eggs	Millicent Selsam	Scott
Egg to Chick		International Press
Play with Leaves and Flowers		Morrow
Play with Plants		Morrow
Play with Trees		Morrow
Play with Vines		Morrow
Anywhere in the World	Irma Webber	Scott
Thanks to Trees		Scott
Travelers All		Scott
Up Above and Down Below		Scott
Frogs and Toads	Herbert S. Zim	Morrow

What's inside of Animals?		Morrow
What's inside of the Earth?		Morrow
What's inside of Me?		Morrow
What's inside of Plants?		Morrow

True-to-Life Animal, Bird, and Weather Stories

All Ready for Winter	Leone Adelson	McKay
Restless Robin	Marjorie Flack	Houghton Mifflin
Tim Tadpole		Doubleday
Wait for the Rain	Martha Goldberg	Holiday
The Big Snow	Berta and Elmer Hader	Macmillan
Go with the Sun	Miriam Shlein	Scott
Time for Sleep	Millicent Selsam	Scott
Billy Goes Exploring	Dorothy Sterling	Doubleday
Sophie and Her Puppies		Doubleday
Baby Jack and Jumping Jack Rabbit	Lloyd Tireman	Univ. of New Mexico
Follow the Wind	Alvin S. Tresselt	Lothrop, Lee & Shepard
Johnny Maple Leaf		Lothrop, Lee & Shepard
Rain Drop Splash		Lothrop, Lee & Shepard
White Snow, Bright Snow		Lothrop, Lee & Shepard
The Storm Book	Zolotow	Harper

Book List for Children Age 8 to 11

General Information

All about Dinosaurs	Roy Chapman Andrews	Random House
My Body and How It Works	Dorothy Baruch	Harper
Experiments in Science	Nelson O. Beeler and Franklyn M. Branley	Crowell
More Experiments in Science		Crowell
Experiments with Electricity		Crowell

Experiments in Chemistry		Crowell
Experiments with Airplane Instruments		Crowell
Dinosaurs	Dorothy Bloch	Coward-McCann
When You Go to the Zoo	Glenn Blough	Whittlesey House
What Makes It Tick?	Katherine Britton	Houghton Mifflin
Wonder World of Ants	Wilfrid S. Bronson	Harcourt, Brace
In Woods and Fields	Margaret Waring Buck	Abingdon
In Yards and Gardens		Abingdon
Big Tree	Conrad and Mary Buff	Viking
First Book of Sea Shells	Betty Cavanna	Watts
First Book of Stones	Maribelle Cormack	Watts
First Book of Trees		Watts
Understanding Science	William Crouse	Whittlesey House
First Book of Plants	Alice Dickinson	Watts
First Book of Prehistoric Animals		Watts
A Book of Nature	Pelagie Doane	Oxford
Sea Shells	Ruth A. Dudley	Crowell
Birds and Their Nests	Olive L. Earle	Morrow
Thunder Wings: The Story of a Ruffed Grouse		Morrow
First Book of Electricity	Sam and Beryl Epstein	Watts
Rocks	Eva Knox Evans	Capitol
Shells		Capitol
Land We Live On	Carroll Lane Fenton and Mildred Adams	Doubleday
Rocks		Doubleday
Worlds in the Sky		John Day
Prehistoric World		John Day
Fun with Astronomy	Mae and Ira Freeman	Random House
Fun with Chemistry		Random House
Fun with Science		Random House
Let's Look at the Stars	Edwin B. Frost	Houghton Mifflin
Real Book of Stars	Hal Goodwin	Garden City
First Book of Snakes	John Hoke	Watts
The Stars for Children	Gaylord Johnson	Macmillan
Strange Visitor (a praying mantis)	Edith F. Johnston	Macmillan

Trees of the Countryside	Margaret McKenny	Knopf
Life through the Ages	Charles Knight	Knopf
All about the Sea	Ferdinand C. Lane	Random House
All about Birds	Robert S. Lemmon	Random House
Picture Book of Astronomy	Jerome S. Meyer	Lothrop, Lee & Shepard
Picture Book of Earth		Lothrop, Lee & Shepard
Picture Book of Weather		Lothrop, Lee & Shepard
Picture Book of Chemistry		Lothrop, Lee & Shepard
Picture Book of Electricity		Lothrop, Lee & Shepard
Picture Book of Molecules and Atoms		Lothrop, Lee & Shepard
The Aquarium Book	Alfred Morgan	Scribner
If You Could See Inside	Marie Neurath	Lothrop, Lee & Shepard
I'll Show You How It Happens		Lothrop, Lee & Shepard
Wonder World of Animals		Lothrop, Lee & Shepard
Wonder World of Birds		Lothrop, Lee & Shepard
Long Ago		Lothrop, Lee & Shepard
First Book of Water	Jo and Ernest Norling	Watts
Golden Book of Natural History	Bertha S. Parker	Simon & Schuster
How Things Work	Creighton Peet	Holt
All about Earthquakes and Volcanoes	Frederick H. Pough	Random House
Junior Book of Birds	Roger Peterson	Houghton Mifflin
Field Guide to Birds	Charles Reed	Doubleday
Homes and Habits of Wild Animals	Karl P. Schmidt	Donohue
My Body and How It Works	Herman and Nina Schneider	Scott
Everyday Weather and How It Works		Whittlesey House

It's Fun to Know Why	Julius Schwartz	Whittlesey House
Through the Magnifying Glass		Whittlesey House
The Zoo	Alberta Semrad	Rand McNally
Weathercraft	A. J. Spilhaus	Viking
All about the Weather	Ray F. Tannehill	Random House
First Book of Bees	Arthur Tibbetts	Watts
Water, Water Everywhere	Mary Walsh	Abingdon
Birds in their Homes	Addison Webb	Garden City
All about the Stars	Anne Terry White	Random House
First Book of Birds	Margaret Williamson	Watts
First Book of Bugs		Watts
Elephants	Herbert F. Zim	Morrow
Gold Fish		Morrow
Golden Hamsters		Morrow
Homing Pigeons		Morrow
Owls		Morrow
Parakeets		Morrow
Rabbits		Morrow
Lightning and Thunder		Morrow
The Sun		Morrow
Birds		Simon & Schuster
Flowers		Simon & Schuster
Insects		Simon & Schuster
Reptiles and Amphibians		Simon & Schuster
Stars		Simon & Schuster
Trees		Simon & Schuster

True-to-Life Stories of Animals

Garden Spider	Mary S. Adrian	Holiday
Honey Bee		Holiday
Fiddler Crab		Holiday
Gray Squirrel		Holiday
Tree on the Road to Turn Town	Glenn O. Blough	Whittlesey House
Not Only for Ducks		Whittlesey House
Wait for the Sunshine		Whittlesey House
Hop, Skip and Fly	Irmengarde Eberle	Holiday

Wagtail	Alice Gall and Fleming Crew	Oxford
Flat Tail		Oxford
Ringtail		Oxford
Winter Flight		Oxford
Tree in the Trail	Holling C. Holling	Houghton Mifflin
Wild World Tales	Henry B. Kane	Knopf
Let Them Live	Dorothy P. Lathrop	Macmillan
Manty, the Mantis	Burr Leyson	Dutton
Monarch Butterfly	Marion Marcher	Holiday
Pogo's House	Jo and Ernest Norling	Holt
Pogo's Mining Trip		Holt
Follow the Sunset	Herman and Nina Schneider	Doubleday
Downy Woodpecker	Paul M. Sears	Holiday
Tree Frog		Holiday
Barn Swallow		Holiday
Snowshoe Twins	Jane Tompkins	Lippincott
The Racoon Twins		Lippincott
The Beaver Twins		Lippincott
The Porcupine Twins		Lippincott
The Otter Twins		Lippincott

Book List for Children Age 12 and Up

General Information

Nature's Ways: How Nature Takes Care of Its Own	Roy Chapman Andrews	Lothrop, Lee & Shepard
Birds of America (short ed.)	John James Audubon	Doubleday
Birds of America (long ed.)		Doubleday
Sound: An Experiment Book	Marian E. Baer	Holiday
When the Stars Come Out	Robert H. Baker	Viking
Electronics for Young People	Jeanne Bendick	Whittlesey House
Atoms at Work	George P. Bischof	Harcourt, Brace
Mars	Franklyn M. Branley	Crowell

Handbook of Nature Study	Anna Comstock	Comstock
Nature Notebook	Robert Candy	Houghton Mifflin
Volcanoes New and Old	Satis Coleman	John Day
Nature Was First	Walter C. Fabell	McKay
Rocks and Their Stories	Carroll Lane Fenton and Mildred Adams	Doubleday
Earth's Adventures		John Day
Life Long Ago		John Day
Riches from the Earth		John Day
Volcano	Tom Galt	Crowell
Story of Sound	James Geralton	Harcourt, Brace
The Insect World	Hilda T. Harpster	Viking
The Animal Book	Dorothy and Nils Hogner	Oxford
The Book of Farm Animals		Oxford
Atoms Today and Tomorrow	Margaret O. Hyde	Whittlesey House
The Story of Trees	Ferdinand C. Lane	Doubleday
All about the Insect World		Random House
All about the Sea		Random House
A Baby Is Born	Milton Levine and Jean Seligman	Simon & Schuster
The Wonder of Life		Simon & Schuster
You and Atomic Energy	John Lewellen	Children's Press
You and Your Amazing Mind		Children's Press
You and Space Neighbors		Children's Press
Animal Clothing	George F. Mason	Morrow
Animal Homes		Morrow
Animal Sounds		Morrow
Animal Tools		Morrow
Animal Tracks		Morrow
Animal Weapons		Morrow
First Chemistry Book for Boys and Girls	Alfred Morgan	Scribner
A First Electrical Book for Boys		Scribner
Stars by Clock and Fist	Henry Neely	Viking

Picture Book of Nature	Samuel Nisenson	Garden City
From Head to Foot	Alex Novikoff	International Press
Field Guide to Birds	Roger Tory Peterson	Houghton Mifflin
Today's Science and You	Lynn Poole	Whittlesey House
Science, the Super Sleuth		Whittlesey House
Diving for Science		Whittlesey House
Snakes Alive	Clifford Pope	Viking
Birds of America	T. Gilbert Pearson	Garden City
Earth for Sam	W. Maxwell Reed	Harcourt, Brace
Sea for Sam		Harcourt, Brace
Stars for Sam		Harcourt, Brace
Patterns in the Sky		Harcourt, Brace
Animals on the March		Harcourt, Brace
Grass: Our Greatest Crop	Sarah C. Reidman	Nelson
Your Blood and You		Abelard-Schuman
Water for People		Abelard-Schuman
A First Book of Tree Identification	Matilda Rogers	Random House
Radar and other Electronic Inventions	Frank J. Ross	Lothrop, Lee & Shepard
Prehistoric Animals	William E. Scheele	World
The First Mammals		World
Everyday Machines and How They Work	Herman and Nina Schneider	Whittlesey House
How Your Body Works		Scott
More Power to You		Whittlesey House
Rocks, Rivers and the Changing Earth		Scott
Bright Design	Katherine B. Shippen	Viking
Men, Microscopes and Living Things		Viking
Trees and Their Uses	Dorothy Sterling	Doubleday
Polio Pioneers		Doubleday
Being Born	Frances Strain	Appleton-Century-Crofts
Boys' Book of Insects	Edwin Way Teale	Dutton

Land Renewed	Wm. R. Van Dersal and E. H. Graham	Oxford
Wild Life for America		Oxford
Gifts from the Forest	Gertrude Wall	Scribner
Dipperful of Stars	Lou Williams	Follett
Planet Earth	Rose Wyler	Abelard-Schuman
Atomic Experiments for Boys	Raymond C. Yates	Harper
Boy and a Battery		Harper
Boy and a Motor		Harper
Boys' Book of Magnets		Harper
Mice, Men and Elephants	Herbert S. Zim	Harcourt, Brace
Minerals		Harcourt, Brace
Plants		Harcourt, Brace

True-to-Life Stories

Quest of the Snow Leopard	Roy Chapman Andrews	Viking
One Day on Beetle Rock	Sally Carrigher	Knopf
Monte	George Franklin	Houghton Mifflin
Tricky		Houghton Mifflin
Sheba		Houghton Mifflin
Wild Animals of the Southwest		Houghton Mifflin
Little Fox	Frances Frost	Whittlesey House
Masked Prowler	John and Jean George	Dutton
Meph		Dutton
Vulpes		Dutton
Vison		Dutton
Rufus	Dorothy Childs Hogner	Lippincott
Chip, the Dam Builder	Jim Kjelgaard	Holiday
Haunt Fox		Holiday
Kalak of the Ice		Holiday
Lion Hound		Holiday
Persimmon	George W. Lippincott	Lippincott
Long Horn		Lippincott
The Phantom Deer		Lippincott

Striped Coat, the Skunk		Lippincott
Wahoo Bobcat		Lippincott
Ben, a Wild Rabbit		Lippincott
Pirate of the North	Harold McCracken	Lippincott
The Great White Buffalo		Lippincott
Sentinel on the Snow Peaks		Lippincott
The Biggest Bear on Earth		Lippincott
Wings in the Woods	Robert McClung	Morrow

6

Books to Help Children Understand and Adjust to the Social World

JUST as important and essential as understanding the physical world and knowing of the great scientific and technical contributions to man's welfare is the sharing of hopes, ideas, and common joys and suffering. Awareness of these factors is equally essential to a growing child's understanding of himself and others. The real goal of the social studies today is to help each child understand how he came to be as he is, how other human beings came to be as they are, and how understanding our common humanity can make it possible for all human beings to fully develop their capacities and live amicably together on the same earth. Such basic human goals offer a more dynamic motivation for all study of mankind than has ever existed before. Geography and history consist not merely of data about places, peoples, wars, and changing ways of living; they contain the very essence of what man lives by and what man lives for.

To live together in such mutual respect and understanding, human beings need to share their thinking, their actual ways of living, and their ideas and ideals—the highest expression of culture. Here, again, the richest resource for the transmitting of such knowledge, ideas, and ideals is books. Those words— put together in truth and beauty, in the past and the present —share man's experience at its best. By reading such books, the child enters into personal experience as well as universal experience. A child knows first the people closest to him—his family. Gradually, the circle widens to include his neighbors, his community, his country, and the world. Books can help him widen this circle.

Books about Ourselves and People

For Children to Age 9

Some of our most beautiful picture books are for children up to the age of nine. They concern happy families and combine fine warm human relations with an understanding of young children. Sometimes these books stem from the family life of the author or author-illustrator. This is true of the two beautiful books by Robert McCloskey, *Blueberries for Sal* and *One Morning in Maine*. These are large books, satisfying both looking and listening needs most effectively if spread on a low table or floor. They are stories of a family living on an island in Maine. The blue used in the type and pictures is the blue of the ocean; it helps the reader feel the local atmosphere. Sal goes out with her mother to gather blueberries. They meet a mother bear and cub who are doing the same thing. *One Morning in Maine* is the story of that exciting morning when Sally lost her first tooth in the mud. She showed the big hole in her mouth to her friend, the grocer, who thought this the occasion for presenting Sally with an ice-cream cone.

Three little children known as "Three Little Steps" are the main characters in a group of gay stories about everyday life. Brightly colored, realistic pictures and the small size of the books add to their appeal. Charlotte Becker is the author-illustrator of:

Three Little Steps
Three Little Steps and the Party (fun at a birthday party)
Three Little Steps and the Snow Dog (winter frolic)
Three Little Steps and the Spotted Horse (a rocking horse meets a long-held desire)

Many children do not like to go to bed because they are afraid they might miss some of the family fun. In *While Susie Sleeps,* Nina Schneider tells the things that most families do in the evening and many things that take place outside at night, such as men bringing milk or bread to the grocery store in preparation for early morning purchases. The pictures in night colors—black, gray, pale yellow—show Susie asleep in her upstairs bedroom and the family downstairs reading, talking, and listening to music.

Juanita by Leo Politi, with a charming text and illustrated in the exquisite pastel colors with which he paints so beautifully, tells the story of a little Mexican girl. Her family call their shop on Olvera Street in Los Angeles "Juanita" after her because they love her so much. It is a spring story, about Juanita's birthday and the exciting day before Easter when the priest in the nearby church blesses all the pets of the children.

Jerrold Beim's stories of everyday family life are easy enough for many first graders and for nearly all second graders to read by themselves. In *Kid Brother,* Frankie proves his worth as a thoughtful brother. In *Tim and the Tool Chest,* Tim learns how to use and take care of his father's tools before he is given a set of his own. There are many more, all well worth reading.

Most families have fun together, but some do not. In Edward Mammen's *The Buttons Go Walking*, the Button family have much fun. If a child comes from a family which does have fun together, he enjoys the Buttons. If the reader comes from a family that does not have fun together, such vicarious experience as offered by this book can give him much joy and satisfaction.

Families are very much alike the world over. Several artists who lived in China enjoyed the family life there so much that they tell delightful stories and draw interesting pictures about it in books. Thomas Handforth's *Mei Li* is the story of a beloved festival in China, New Year's day. Just by looking at the pictures of the mother, one knows she is a good mother. That she is a mother is more important than that she is a Chinese woman. Grandmother, coming to visit her three grandchildren, brings them each a present and gives them a penny to spend in *Wu and Lu and Li*, by Evelyn Young, just like grandmothers the world over. In Yen Liang's *Tommy and Dee Dee*, it is good to find out how much alike American Tommy and Chinese Dee Dee are.

Ann Nolan Clark's third grade Tesuque Indian children told her much about their family life. In poetic prose she tells their story: *In My Mother's House*. A distinguished Indian artist Herrera drew the characteristic Indian pictures.

Herman and Nina Schneider show how much alike families are the world around in their book, *Follow the Sunset*. The sun is setting in eastern United States. Fathers come home, children get ready for the evening meal, mother prepares that meal, they all go to bed while mother sings a lullaby. As the earth turns, the sunset hour comes to families who live in widely differing places, dress differently, and eat different food, but all of whom welcome father, share an evening meal, and go to their rest.

Some families live on farms in the country. Any reader can

share farm life in *Willy's Farm* by the Hurds, or observe in detail the changes of the four seasons in the books about Meadowbrook Farm by Katherine Keelor:

Spring Comes to Meadowbrook Farm
Summer Comes to Meadowbrook Farm
Autumn Comes to Meadowbrook Farm
Winter Comes to Meadowbrook Farm

Other families live in towns and cities. The Petershams show the sights of the city and describe the people who live there in *The Big City*. They deal similarly with a typical small town in *Little Town*. Phyllis McGinley takes children all over a town to see everything and everybody in *All Around the Town*. She does it with an alphabet: "P" is the Proud Policeman; "B," the Bus. Helen Stone's pictures make the book beautiful.

A little cat goes up in a balloon in *The Noon Balloon* and floats over farms, meadows, rivers, and cities. He sees and hears and feels the different sights and sounds of each in the beautiful poetic prose of Margaret Wise Brown. Many more of her books are very close to the heart of a child.

In every child's life, the first experiences in school make great advances in widening the circle of people he knows well. Most children love to read about school experiences just like their own. Second graders usually can read:

Speckles Goes to School	Martha Goldberg
(Speckles is a hen.)	
The Lunch Box Story	Grace Berquist
The School Bus Picnic	Aaron Fine

These longer stories are enjoyed more by third and fourth graders:

The School Train	Helen Acker
Here Comes the School Train	William Bunce
B Is for Betsy	Carolyn Haywood
Back to School with Betsy	
Two and Two Are Four	
First Grade	Eleanor Lattimore
Lucky Days for Johnny	Irene Smith

As children begin to play baseball and other group games, they have to learn how to be part of a team, how to act for the good of many instead of for only themselves, how to lose as well as win, how to become what we call a "good sport." The stories of Terry and Bunky by Fishel are not only good stories about the boys but also give most of the basic rules of each game:

Terry and Bunky Play Baseball
Terry and Bunky Play Football
Terry and Bunky Play Basketball

Christopher's *The Lucky Baseball Bat* not only tells the story of a boy's adjustment to strange boys but also has something to say about luck as a thing to depend on. Marion Renick tells good stories about sports and points up the transition from self-centeredness to interest and willingness to play with others in all her books. These are a few of her books:

The Heart for Baseball
Jimmy's Own Basketball
Micky's Football Team
Pete's Home Run

Coming to know people who live near their homes, visiting with the older ones, and playing with the younger ones extends children's acquaintance to many people, some of whom may be quite different from themselves and their families. *Two Is a Team* by Jerrold Beim, tells of two little boys who each try to build a wagon alone. Neither wagon is very good, so they build one together. This one proves to be good enough for them to make deliveries for the grocer. They go to the home of one of the boys, a negro; the boys are friends. *Nappy Wanted a Friend* by Inez Hogan is also the story of friendship between a negro boy and a white boy. Three charming stories by Lavinia Davis, *Wild Birthday Cake, Roger and the Fox,* and *Danny's Luck,* are stories of small boys and their neighbors. Hildegarde Woodward's illustrations add greatly to the beauty of these books.

Ruth Benedict and Gene Weltfish, anthropologists, have a delightful book of cartoons, *Bill and His Neighbors*, about a variety of people of all races who have much in common.

There are an increasing number of books about the activities and services of communities. Markets and stores are exciting places in which to shop. Marjorie Medary's *Store at Criss Cross Corners* and Jerrold Beim's *Country Store* are good stories about small stores. Olds' *Kristy and the Frosty Packages* takes the reader right into a supermarket. It is longer than the other two, better for third and fourth grade reading. In *Market Day for Ti Andre*, Maia Rodman makes a colorful Haitiian market really come alive. Any small reader will really think Seth is lucky to be able to help his uncle at the filling station in *Country Garage* by Jerrold Beim. Leonard Weisgard's pictures give extra appeal to a story of things that stop and go by Golden MacDonald: *Red Light, Green Light*.

A policeman is everybody's friend. Every child will think so more than ever as he reads *Make Way for Ducklings* by Robert McCloskey and sees the policeman hold back traffic on a crowded Boston street to allow a mother duck to get her ducklings safely across to a pond in the Common. Tim felt that next to his father, Mike, the policeman at the corner where he turned to go to school, was his best friend. He was sure of it when Mike and Tim's dog Brownie really saved Tim's life the morning of the marble tournament in *Tim and the Brass Buttons* by Ruth Tooze. Many of its readers say, "Tim could have been me." Identification such as this offers genuine learning opportunities.

The Martin family really had fun together, including the time they spent with hobbies. Bird-watching was a favorite, so John was much disappointed the night after Christmas when his father had to go off on a long trip, just after they had set up their new bird feeder. The purple martins in early spring, a broken telephone wire, John's birthday, and his dad's return all build up to a moment of real suspense in this story *Wires Up!* by Ruth Tooze. Keeping wires up in a family where rapport

between its members is good, is as important as keeping telephone wires up so people can talk to each other when necessary.

Through constant association with books like these, children
truly learn how to get along with others and understand themselves better; their needs for fun and beauty, knowledge and
adventure are satisfied. Children will read these books if they
are easily available, returning to them again and again, because
they are a satisfying extension of their own experience. The
few discussed here are only a small portion of the large number with which it is good for children to live.

As a child grows, his horizons widen. Adequate understanding of himself and others necessitates going back in time and
across countless miles to know all kinds of people. In the past
are his forebears. Their patterns of living, their desires, their
decisions affect his whole being—his pattern of living, his desires, his decisions. A child who is growing up in America is
likely to find the history of America's development especially
interesting. The story of his country need not be a dull suc-
cession of important events, elections, and wars. It can be as exciting in the reading as in the living; vicarious experience can
almost take children there. People came from all over the world
to build America, so this adventure of reliving the past must
take the child back in time to other lands, especially those
from which so many people came, seeking freedom or new opportunity.

During the past eras, when communication and transportation were less highly developed, many countries and nations
lived almost wholly within themselves. For centuries, peoples
on different continents did not know each other and did not
care about anyone but themselves. So it was that American
study of history, until recently, gave little attention to the
Orient or Africa. We studied American history, European history, ancient Greek and Roman, ancient Egyptian, primarily
because we felt our heritage came from these people. This was

true until fairly recently, despite Marco Polo's adventure in far Cathay, despite the significance of the East India company. But this is changing as the world draws closer together. The influence of every nation upon every other, the exchange of philosophies as well as goods becomes increasingly evident. So, in our time, when the nations of the world are interdependent economically, politically, philosophically, and spiritually, every growing child needs to be aware of all people everywhere; they are his friends and neighbors. Suffering, poverty, or lack of privilege in one area of the world affects every other area, even those of greater privilege and ease of living. An increasing number of books of both fact and fiction have been published for children in recent years. Through them they know people all over the world—how they live and what they mean to growing Americans.

Nonfiction with a "New Look"

There is a wealth of nonfiction with a "new look," with real human interest, not just an assembling of factual information. There are several beginning anthropologies. *All about Us* and *People Are Important* by Eva Knox Evans are easy to read, and they arouse interest in and bring appreciation of all the ways in which people are different as well as those in which they are alike. Children who find these of interest will want to go on to read *The Big Family of Peoples* by Eberle, *The Growing Human Family* by Masani, *Races and People* by Asimov and Boyd and *Four Ways of Being Human* by Lisitzky.

As American children begin the adventure of discovering how their country grew, they are fascinated by Mabel Pyne's two large, flat books, *The Little Geography of the United States* and *The Little History of the United States*. In the geography, the approach in terms of what it is like to live on the plains, in the mountains, in river valleys, reveals the influence of land upon people as well as that of people upon land. The skillful selection of high peaks of history accompanied by lively line drawings in the *Little History* holds the attention of children at all ages. Two page spreads picturing the explorers as well as illustrating the interesting story take exploring children along in Alice Dalgliesh's *America Begins*. They feel quite at home with early settlers in her book *America Builds Homes* and with the early Dutch in *Wooden Shoes in America*.

As children grow older, the meaning of geography becomes more evident. Perhaps a choral speaking group will want to use the rhythmic informative text of Fenton's *The Land We Live On*, thus making an interesting group experience that goes beyond individual reading. Part of the group might show the excellent photographs in a reflector or even make slides from them. This paves the way for almost everyone's wanting to read *Why We Live Where We Live*, Evans' book telling how the shape of the land—the harbors, rivers, and lakes; the mountains, plains, and prairies—affect each one of us. *Know Your U.S.A.* gives basic information about each state and depicts great moments in our country's growing in colorful sketches, graphs, and brief, clear text. Kohl and Nisenson in *Your America* do a similar thing by a quite different means. In this book, each state, each person, each event, is personal and seems to be talking in self-explanation. McFall's *Our Country America* is another book with few words and effective sketches, graphs, and charts. It may well be the first of a new type of book in which the graphic presentation plays as important a role as the text in presenting this nation, what it gets from the earth, what it makes, what it sends out, what it imports, the nature of our government, our cultural life, and other exciting aspects of our country. The child who really finds how rewarding such reading can be as he comes to the upper grades will be eager to find out more about the motives and drives that lay back of the exploration, colonization, and growth of the Western Hemisphere.

Baity's *America Before Man* and White's *Prehistoric Amer-*

ica really take their readers back in time to earliest beginnings. *Americans Before Columbus,* also by Baity, reveals with its beautiful photographs the early Incan and Mayan civilizations at the height of their glory. Many a child who reads this will have a greater respect for the Indians of the Western Hemisphere. Real exploration is possible for the child who reads *New Found World* by Shippen and *Vast Horizons* by Lucas. Here is the way Katherine Shippen opens doors:[1]

> A new art has been born in Latin America. It has the grace of the Mayans, and the strength of the Aztecs, and the piety of candles on Spanish altars. It has the soft cadences of Spanish speech, and the melancholy wisdom of the Indian. See how painting and poetry, music and dance, all blend together in a new design.

Some children "discover" an author and then want to read everything he or she writes. It is a real adventure to "discover" Katherine Shippen and through her find history made alive. The discoverer will be eager to read *The Great Heritage,* a human and scholarly appraisal of our heritage from the land and from the men before us. *I Know a City,* the superbly told story of the growth of the city of New York, is interesting not only to New Yorkers but to all Americans. *Passage to America* is a rich narrative of people and incidents that have gone into the making of America. The stamp collector will find the whole pageant of American history recreated in *Commemorative Stamps of the U.S.A.* by Reinfeld.

A group of books known as *Landmark books* present history —fact not fiction—in a colorful and inviting way, with skillful selection from authoritative sources and an excellent format. The choice of type as well as double spacing of the lines helps readability. Many outstanding authors of adult books have brought their literary talents to the writing of these books; reading them is likely to whet the appetite for more reading. Here are only a few of these new, dynamic accounts of explora-

[1] Katherine Shippen, in *New Found World* (New York: Viking, 1945), p. 239.

tion and dramatic development in American government, trade, and communication:

The Vikings	Elizabeth Janeway
The Voyages of Christopher Columbus	Armstrong Sperry
The Landing of the Pilgrims	James Daugherty
The Winter at Valley Forge	Van Wyck Mason
Our Independence and the Constitution	Dorothy Canfield Fisher
The Barbary Pirates	C. S. Forester
The Louisiana Purchase	Robert Tallant
Clipper Ship Days	John Jennings
The Lewis and Clark Expedition	Richard Neuberger
The Pony Express	Samuel Hopkins Adams
Custer's Last Stand	Quentin Reynolds
Lee and Grant at Appommatox	MacKinlay Kantor

When the time comes to understand more clearly just how our government functions, Elting's *We Are the Government* and Holisher's *Capitol Hill* give their readers a vivid picture of the functioning and interrelationship of all departments. Wagner's *Put Democracy to Work* presents a comprehensive picture of the basic principles of American democracy traced from the Magna Charta to the present.

Too often we study history in sections, not seeing the important relationships or the on-moving sweep of the growth pattern. Genevieve Foster presents a cross-section of the whole world at a specific period of time in several of her books such as *Augustus Caesar's World, George Washington's World,* and *Abraham Lincoln's World.* The narrative of what was going on in China, Germany, Russia, France, and North Africa, while people were building America is exciting reading; it helps one see things in perspective. Because she is an artist, there are many attractive line drawings, often in two-page spreads, that will intrigue a child of ten or eleven and lead older children to follow through with reading. Is it any wonder that the reading child in the United States of America shares his country's growth experiences as he sees and relives its land development, its people's struggles, its expansion, its economic and cultural growth? Surely, as he grows to the age at which he accepts a citizen's responsibility, he acquires some understanding and a mind and heart open for further development. The struggles of many people in many parts of the world for the right to live their own lives in their own way is creating new nations such as Pakistan. It is shifting the center of more active development from the Atlantic to the Pacific basin, and is making all nations more interdependent economically and culturally. Every child in every nation needs to know about not only his own people and country, but all people and countries. Perhaps the American child needs wider knowledge and deeper understanding than those of some other countries because of the position of leadership his country occupies today.

Every government functions within the framework of the people's interests. Therefore, one path to understanding lies along the way of sharing those interests in work; in expression through art, music, and literature; in patterns of living. In all countries, tradition and the new ways press against each other, each modifying the other. Many changing ways of many nations with changed names and governments have not even found their way into the social studies texts frequently still used in schools today. Thus, books about the world as it is and what it is becoming have a unique significance.

Skill in selecting essential facts and aspects of a people's growth, emphasis upon human values, objectivity, and colorful illustrations or photographs characterize the new nonfiction about many nations of the world.

For younger children there are a group of large size picture books in which history marches across the pages; here today's children can become friends and neighbors:

Picture Story of China	Emily Hahn
Picture Story of France	Clarke Hutton
Picture Story of Hawaii	Hester O'Neill
Picture Story of Holland	Dola De Jong
Picture Story of Sweden	Hester O'Neill

For children in the middle grades there are several excellent series of books about other lands, such as Vernon Quinn's picture geographies, Lippincott's *Portraits of the Nations* series, Holiday House's *Lands and People* series, *The First Book of Japan* by Mears, *The First Book of Israel* by Kubie, *First Book of India* by Hahn, and *First Book of Mexico* by Epstein. *Getting to Know Korea*, *Getting to Know Germany*, and *Getting to Know Puerto Rico* by Tor, and *The Mexican Story* by McNeer, beautifully illustrated by Lynd Ward, also provide excellent reading material for this age group.

The Vernon Quinn Picture Geographies

Pageant of the Seven Seas
Picture Map of Africa
Picture Map Geography of Asia
Picture Map Geography of Canada and Alaska
Picture Map Geography of Mexico, Central America and West Indies
Picture Map Geography of South America
Picture Map Geography of the United States

Portraits of Nations Series

Land of William of Orange	Barnouw
Land of Joan of Arc	Bragdon
Land of William Tell	
Land and People of Brazil	Brown
Land and People of Greece	Gianapoulis
Land and People of Israel	Hoffman
Land of the Polish People	Kelly
Land and People of Mexico	Larralda
Land and People of India	Modak
Land and People of Sweden	Nano
Land of the Russian People	Nazaroff
Land and People of Ireland	O'Brien
Land and People of South Africa	Paton
Land and People of Canada	Ross
Land of the Chinese People	Spencer

Land of the English People	Street
Land and People of Japan	Vaughan
Land of the Italian People	Winwar

Lands and Peoples Series

Arab Lands	Brittain
Australia	Busoni
Brazil	Kenworthy
British Isles	Sloane
Dutch East Indies	De Leeuw
Egypt	Taylor
France	Davis
Germany	Berner
Iran	Taylor
Italy	Busoni
Japan	Spencer
Low Countries	Spencer
Mexico	Busoni
Oceania	Borden
Scandinavia	Evans
Turkey	Ives
Yugoslavia	Kish

Some of the Landmark series mentioned above are concerned with building clearer world understanding, for example:

Genghis Khan and the Mongol Horde	Harold Lamb
The Battle of Britain	Quentin Reynolds
Adventures and Discoveries of Marco Polo	Richard J. Walsh
The Crusades	Anthony West
Queen Elizabeth and the Spanish Armada	Frances Winwar

Another group of books is by people who have lived in each land and illustrated their books with photographs of strong human interest:

Turkey Old and New	Selma Ekrem
Here Is the Veldt	Attilio Gatti
Mediterranean Spotlights	
Here Is Africa	Ellen and Attilio Gatti
Here Is India	Jean Kennedy

It is interesting to note how areas that are growing in importance in today's world are the first to be presented in these various books giving world background.

As Japan faced the problem of finding a new place in the family of nations and of building for itself a nation based upon a democratic way of life, its emperor decided that his son—the crown prince—needed some instruction from a teacher of insight and wisdom. He chose Elizabeth Gray Vining, an American. She tells about her experience of teaching the prince in *Windows for the Crown Prince*. The book will "open windows" for every young person who reads it.

In *A World Full of Homes*, Burns gives a fascinating account of the ingenious ways in which man has used the basic materials he could find or manufacture to shelter himself and his family from rain and snow, heat and cold. Batchelor answers many questions about human communication from its simple beginning to its more modern complex forms in *Communication: From Cave Writing to Television*.

Ever since the time of Christ, men have been increasingly concerned with the brotherhood of man and better world understanding. Political and religious experiments have come and gone, failing for the most part because of selfishness, will to power, or inadequate knowledge and understanding. One of the most sincere experiments made so far is that of the United Nations. Whether it survives or dies to rise phoenix-like in some other form, today's young people should understand its ways of working. They will grow in human understanding as they read these books:

Workshops for the World	Graham Beckel
A Fair World for All: The Meaning of the Declaration of Human Rights	Dorothy Canfield Fisher
How The United Nations Works	Tom Galt
Partners: The United Nations and Youth	Roosevelt and Ferris
The Pool of Knowledge	Katherine Shippen
United Nations, New York	Dorothy Sterling

A world to know, children eager to know it, books that make it real and significant! Perhaps putting these forces together will help prepare the children who must soon assume responsibility in this world.

Biography

Probably one of the other good ways to understanding is through knowing the distinguished people whose decisions, actions, and lives have determined the growth or recession of nations. Perhaps this generation owes a special debt of gratitude to Lytton Strachey for writing a new kind of biography. Some called it *debunking*, for it was a far cry from the old type of eulogy or assemblage of cold facts. To face shortcomings honestly, to tell of significant achievements makes the subject of the biography seem human and real. Biography today, for children and young people as well as adults, has become alive, warm, human. Children may truly feel that some of their best friends are famous people.

Even for comparatively young children, there are appealing picture biographies such as *Daniel Boone* by Esther Averill and the group by Edgar and Ingri d'Aulaire. The beautiful stone lithographs of the d'Aulaires enhance the life story of each hero in *Leif the Lucky, George Washington, Abraham Lincoln, Benjamin Franklin, Pocahontas,* and *Christopher Columbus.* The d'Aulaires live with their heroes for a long time by reading books about them, by visiting the places where these heroes have lived. Then follows much discussion of all the assembled facts and a sympathetic selection of just the high spots that are likely to appeal most to the interested child. No wonder that such writing and drawing as theirs, growing out of living experience, lives on and on and enables readers to relive the experiences of the heroes. Jeanette Eaton also recreates the boy and man in *Washington, the Nation's First Hero,* a brief, dramatic story of the first president's life. She does the same in *Robert E. Lee.*

By the time children are nine or ten, most of them can read whatever they are interested in. Pictures still help to hold interest, so the books of the artist-historian, Genevieve Foster, have a double appeal by virtue of charming sketches and two page spreads which picture high dramatic moments in addition to the lively text. She chose four presidents to so interpret: *George Washington, Andrew Jackson, Abraham Lincoln,* and *Theodore Roosevelt.*

Striking illustrations, authentic text, and beautiful format characterize this group of biographies by distinguished historians:

America's Robert E. Lee	Henry Steele Commager
America's Paul Revere	Esther Forbes
America's Ethan Allen	Stewart Holbrook

With increasing realization of both the interest in biography and the value of the biographical approach to the study of history, certain publishing houses are producing groups of books about outstanding people. One of these groups for the middle-grade children is the *Makers of America Books.* Here, again, lives are dramatically retold so that each hero becomes an exciting person to know.

George Washington, First President	Elsie Ball
Christopher Columbus, Discoverer	Alberta Powell Graham
Lafayette, Friend of America	
La Salle, River Explorer	
The Wright Brothers	Haines and Movill
William Penn, Founder and Friend	Virginia Haviland
Leif Ericson, Explorer	Ruth Cromer Weir
Thomas Alva Edison, Inventor	
Sam Houston, Fighter and Leader	Frances Fitzpatrick Wright

Another group is called *Signature Books, the Life Stories of Great People.* They are written by a variety of excellent authors, and edited by Enid Meadowcroft who also wrote some of them. Here are a few of this interesting, readable group:

George Washington Carver	Arna Bontemps
Kit Carson	Edmund Collier
Pocahontas	Shirley Graham
Florence Nightingale	Margaret Leighton
Crazy Horse	Enid Meadowcroft
Davy Crockett	
Martha Washington	Jeanette Covert Nolan
Marco Polo	Olive Price
Daniel Boone	William O. Steele
Robert E. Lee	Iris Vinton

Somehow, most of the biographies written first for children are about the explorers and political leaders of our country. But authors and musicians have also been makers of America. Stephen Foster put into song the feelings of the people moving westward, ever westward, as our country expanded. Catherine Peare has a rare gift for interpreting some of these cultural leaders for ten- and eleven-year-olds:

Stephen Foster: His Life
John James Audubon: His Life
Henry Wadsworth Longfellow: His Life
Louisa May Alcott: Her Life
Robert Louis Stevenson: His Life

Two music teachers, Opal Wheeler and Sybil Deucher, enriched their pupils' backgrounds for music appreciation with stories of the early lives of many of the musicians whose works the children were studying. They have put these life stories, with some of the music of each which a child is likely to know first, into a group of delightful biographies:

Mozart, the Wonder Boy	Wheeler and Deucher
Joseph Haydn: The Merry Little Peasant	
Sebastian Bach: The Boy from Thuringia	
Franz Schubert and His Merry Little Friends	
Edward MacDowell and His Cabin in the Pines	Opal Wheeler
Handel at the Court of Kings	
Ludwig Beethoven and the Chiming Tower Bells	

Stephen Foster and His Little Dog Tray
Robert Schumann and Mascot Ziff
Frederic Chopin, Son of Poland: Early Years
Frederic Chopin, Son of Poland: Later Years
Paganini, Master of Strings
The Story of Peter Tschaikowsky: Early Years
Edvard Grieg, Boy of the Northland   Sybil Deucher
The Young Brahms

Besides all these musicians, there are:

Hans Andersen, Son of Denmark   Opal Wheeler
Giotto Tended the Sheep   Wheeler and Deucher
Millet Tilled the Soil

Collins' *Young Hans Christian Andersen* is another life story
not to miss.

When it comes to biographies of outstanding people for
more mature readers, the quality and quantity is almost overwhelming. One can only mention a few and encourage all
young people as well as their parents and teachers to explore
the biography shelves in school and public libraries, in every
nearby bookstore, to find untold treasure, theirs for the taking.

Many of the Landmark books referred to above introduce
the reader to great people such as:

Daniel Boone   John Mason Brown
The Man Who Changed China: The   Pearl Buck
   Story of Sun Yat-Sen
Ben Franklin of Old Philadelphia   Margaret Cousins
Wild Bill Hickok Tames the West   Stewart Holbrook
John James Audubon   Margaret and John Kieran
Dolly Madison   Jane Mayer
Thomas Jefferson, Father of   Vincent Sheehan
   Democracy
John Paul Jones, Fighting Soldier   Armstrong Sperry
The Wright Brothers   Quentin Reynolds
Napoleon and the Battle   Frances Winwar
   of Waterloo

Another gifted interpreter of five of our great Presidents is Clara Ingram Judson. Many children feel closer to these men through reading their life stories:

Abraham Lincoln: Friend of the People
George Washington: Leader of the People
Theodore Roosevelt: Fighting Patriot
Thomas Jefferson: Champion of the People

The Messner biographical bookshelf now numbers over one hundred titles meeting almost any interest: sports, science, medicine, history, music, literature. These may become friends:

The First Woman Doctor: The Story of Elizabeth Blackwell	Rachel Baker
Sigmund Freud	
Father Junipero Serra	Ivy Bolton
Heroes of the Kalevala	Babette Deutsch
Walt Whitman	
Winged Moccasins: The Story of Sacajawea	Frances Farnsworth
Chief Joseph of the Nez Perces	Shannon Garst
Jack London	
George Washington Carver	Shirley Graham
Your Most Humble Servant (Benjamin Bauneker)	
Louis Braille: Windows for the Blind	J. Alvin Kugelmass
Ralph J. Bunche	
Albert Einstein	Elma E. Levinger
Anton Dvorak	Claire Purdy
He Heard America Sing (Stephen Foster)	
Song of the North (Edvard Grieg)	
The Jim Thorpe Story	Gene Schoor
Red Grange	
Michael Faraday: From Errand Boy to Master Physicist	Harry Sootin
Walter Reed	Wood

One of the most dramatic interpreters of outstanding people, both in the vigor of his pictures and the vitality of his story, is James Daugherty. Many of his books are wonderful to read aloud. The reader can be deeply moved, for here reading becomes living:

Abraham Lincoln
Daniel Boone
Marcus and Narcissa Whitman
Of Courage Undaunted (Lewis and Clark)
Poor Richard

Living with these great leaders may well kindle the spark of faith and courage needed in our frontier time of growth in scientific discovery and world understanding.

Katherine Shippen is another of those interpreters of the past who kindle a flame in her biographies as well as her histories:

Leif Eriksson
Moses

Marguerite Vance has a rare gift of bringing great women of the past close to the girl of today in her books:

Elizabeth Tudor, Sovereign Lady
Lady Jane Grey, Reluctant Queen
Marie Antoinette: Daughter of an Empress
Martha, Daughter of Virginia
On Wings of Fire: Rose Hawthorne

Cecil Woodham-Smith stirs a girl's emotions and evokes admiration for Florence Nightingale in her biography *Lonely Crusader: The Life of Florence Nightingale.* Catherine Peare again reveals her sensitive understanding of a great man in her biography of *Albert Einstein.*

The young person with musical interests will find many of the biographies of great musicians especially appealing:

Richard Wagner Who Followed a Star	Gladys Burch
George Gershwin	David Ewen
Haydn: A Good Life	
Beethoven, Master Musician	Madeleine Goss
Deep Flowing Brook (Bach)	

Unfinished Symphony: Schubert
Brahms the Master   Goss and Schauffler
John Philip Sousa   Anna Lingg
Mephisto Waltz: Franz Liszt
Mozart: Genius of Harmony
My Brother Was Mozart   Wheeler and Deucher

Elizabeth Ripley interprets four of the greatest artists chiefly through their paintings in her books:

Leonardo da Vinci
Michelangelo
Rembrandt
Vincent Van Gogh

When the story of this century comes to be written, probably one of the great persons to know will be Albert Schweitzer—musician, missionary, physician, scientist, philosopher. Joseph Gollomb feels the impact of this great interpreter of Bach on the organ, this unselfish missionary in Africa, this understanding philosopher, and he communicates it in his *Albert Schweitzer*. Manton's *Story of Albert Schweitzer* is another fine picture of this great man.

A unique variety of leaders—Gandhi, Bunche, Schweitzer, Eleanor Roosevelt, and others—are shaping the destinies of men and nations in the twentieth century. Leonard Kenworthy's sincere efforts, through teaching and writing, to develop world-minded young citizens introduces some of history's most important people in *Twelve Citizens of the World*.

The counsel received by a young person in early adolescence frequently determines not only his career but his attitudes and values. Following a discussion by a group of educators about such moments in life, Robert Patterson selected some portions from the autobiographies of representative Americans growing up in various backgrounds and periods of the United States to create the book *On Our Way: Young Pages from American Autobiography*. Alice Hazeltine has compiled another such anthology from autobiographies of Americans from North,

South, East, and West in *We Grew Up in America*. These people represent widely differing backgrounds, early experience, and occupations, and capture the spirit of American growth—its ambitions, disappointments and triumphs. Possibly no reading experience can help young people develop a purpose in their own lives as well as that which gives understanding of how people and their times shape each other. Reading the life stories of people of destiny provides such experience.

Fiction with Historic Background

The increase during recent years in adult historic fiction recreating the past has had its counterpart in historic fiction for children and young people. Probably this is one of the best ways to clothe the skeleton of history outlines with flesh and blood. Even eight- and nine-year-olds may participate in such adventure out of the past. Sparked by an episode related in the Plymouth diary, Elizabeth Coatsworth wrote an adventure story, a dog story, an Indian story, and a history story—all rolled into one—in *The First Adventure*. She has a whole group now of these Once-Upon-a-Time-in-America stories highlighting episodes about fifty years apart. *The Wishing Pear* is about Peter Stuyvesant's pear tree; *Boston Bells* describe John Copley, in Boston at the time of the famous Tea Party. *Aunt Flora* tells about the magnetic Flora MacDonald who came to plead the Stuart cause with her Scotch relatives in North Carolina; *Old Whirlwind* is about the tall-talking hero, Davy Crockett; *The Sod House* relates the story of a family who came from Germany to settle in Kansas.

Miriam Mason has a true gift for storytelling. Children are fortunate that she uses some of it to recreate pioneer days so vividly in *Susannah*, the pioneer cow; *The Sugarbush Family*, the King family who had not much money but plenty of fun; *The Middle Sister*, who took her apple tree clear out to Minnesota; *Caroline and Her Kettle Named Maud*, wherein the kettle, not a gun, saves this little pioneer. These are only a few of her many books.

Not enough of us know how Lafayette, the gay young French general, long after his return to France helped Nantucket through trying days by buying their whale oil when modern inventions were causing a decrease in its use in America. The grateful islanders expressed their gratitude by sending him a 500-pound cheese of their own making. The Marquis and his wife and their children all liked it. They say even the French mice did, too! Elizabeth Meg tells this delightful episode in our history in *A Cheese for Lafayette*.

Each year as Thanksgiving Day comes, children want to know how we came to celebrate this day. There are two appealing stories of its origin:

The First Thanksgiving   Lena Barksdale
The Thanksgiving Story   Alice Dagliesh

Books like these should be a part of the growing-up experience of every small American. Once a child reaches the age at which he can read whatever he wants to, the range in historic fiction is very wide. There are literally hundreds to choose from. Perhaps no stories of any type have been taken by American children more closely to their hearts than those of Laura Ingalls Wilder. These eight books about the Ingalls family from *Little House in the Big Woods* to *These Happy Golden Years* are a genuine saga of American pioneer life. Their simplicity is almost stark, their joys and sorrows so sincere that each reader becomes a very part of the Ingalls family.

Or, perhaps, a child may sense and savor high peaks of his country's growing in the sincere, vivid writing of Enid Meadowcroft. He may become a part of the story *Ship Boy with Columbus*; live through *The First Year* with the Pilgrims, suffer through the winter at Valley Forge in *Silver for General Washington*; come down the Ohio river with the Burd family in *By Wagon and Flatboat*; experience all the excitement of

David's seeking out Jim, a slave who has lost his certificate of freedom back in 1860, and the two boys' exciting homeward trip to Chicago via the underground in *By Secret Railway;* go over the wilderness trails to old Kentucky in *Our Indian Trails with Daniel Boone;* or join the Blake children homesteading in Texas in their exciting adventures with both Indians and Texas Rangers in *Texas Star.*

Little Johann received the name of Johnny from the stage driver that first morning when he arrived in Galveston, Texas, from Hamburg, Germany, and he felt that life in Texas would be "exciting and good like fresh bread and butter when you are hungry." So it proved to be for him and may be for all who read his story in *Johnny Texas* and *Johnny Texas on the San Antonio Road,* both by Carol Hoff.

Settling the far Northwest meant many trials and tribulations as well as joys and excitement in covered wagon days, as one finds out with the *Children of the Covered Wagon* by Mary Carr. One discovers how the four Bounces from New England acquire the whole town of Cynthianna, Oregon, in *The Bounces of Cynthiann'* by Evelyn Lampman. She also makes Seenie Luelling a friend on that trek with the wagon carrying the first grafted fruit trees to Oregon in *Tree Wagon.* Nancy Barnes makes pioneering in Colorado in the early 1900's gay as well as full of hard work in *The Wonderful Year.* Every child who stands to sing with heartwarming fervor the Star-Spangled Banner will cherish Carl Carmer's true story of how the flag that flew over Fort McHenry was made and of the events that morning when it inspired Francis Scott Key to write those words in his book *A Flag for the Fort.* So, too, will they enjoy reading how Yankee Doodle came to be so popular a song in *Hay Foot, Straw Foot* by Erick Berry. Or, it may be thrilling to go far back in time with an Egyptian boy in *Boy of the Pyramids* by Ruth Fosdick Jones.

Robin, crippled after his parents' departure, is cared for by Brother John and ultimately helps save the besieged castle of

We read about the airplanes we build.

It's fun to read.

We find out about other people.

We really live in the past when we read these stories of long ago.

his father's friend because he can swim to the door in the wall. Children may find doors in their own walls when they read his poignant story in *Door in the Wall*, a story of medieval England by Marguerite di Angeli. Watson's stirring story of a highland girl's courage in aiding her Bonnie Prince Charlie makes real the Stuart cause in *Highland Rebel*.

The riches continue in longer stories which are almost full-bodied novels for older readers. *Johnny Tremaine* pays a heavy price for being rather "smarty" over his ability as a silversmith's apprentice, but he serves his country well in the first days of the war following the Boston Tea Party. Esther Forbes tells his story with inside understanding in the book of that name. Stephanie held close the tiny apple seeds as her family, the Venables, trekked over into old Kaintuck. When she planted them, they grew into a tree that became not only a thing of beauty but a symbol of new-found freedom in Rebecca Caudill's moving story *Tree of Freedom*. In *Rebel Siege* by Jim Kjelgaard, that inimitable story-teller recreates the exciting revolutionary war experience of a Carolina riflemaker and his son who helped turn back the British at King's Mountain in 1780.

Felix Holt has adapted his *Gabriel Horn* for young people. Eloise McGraw is becoming a name that makes readers eager for each new book, so vividly does she take them into the experience of her characters. This is especially true of her gripping tale of the Northwest, *Moccasin Trail*. One of the most exciting historic novels in recent years is her *Mara: Daughter of the Nile*, with its picturesque details of the varied life of ancient Egypt in the courts, in shops and inns, on the river boats. Its complex plot involves princes, queens, and a slave girl—half villain, half heroine, but utterly appealing. It is thrilling to go back in time through such reading. Elizabeth Meigs takes her readers each step of the way along the strange path of little Joan, who heard voices and followed their bidding in *Candle in the Sky*, a moving story of Joan of Arc.

Elizabeth Gray makes real the life of a minstrel in medieval England in *Adam of the Road*. Eleanore Jewett recreates the whole pattern of life in an English cathedral at the time of the crusades in *Hidden Treasure of Glaston*. She makes the story even more appealing by setting it in the cathedral wherein legend says Joseph of Arimathea hid the Holy Grail. Marchette Chute can make anyone feel she knew Shakespeare, such is her vast authentic knowledge of the Elizabethan age and her skillful charm of recreating people. Her *Introduction to Shakespeare* offers a rare experience, while *The Wonderful Winter* is a delight as the reader runs away with young Sir Robert Wakefield from three overbearing aunts and a tedious tutor. He makes friends in London with the actor John Hemminge who takes him into his home and the theatre itself. Many young people who saw *How Green Was My Valley* have wanted to read anything by Richard Llewellyn, but have not felt equal to reading a long adult novel. They will eagerly return to picturesque Wales, which always seems to have an eerie bit of coast as well as green valleys whereon witchery is cast, in his *Witch of Merthyn* —a novel written for young people. Romance and history combine to make Cortez' cruel conquering of the great Montezuma in Mexico an exciting adventure to share in Lobdell's *Golden Conquest*. They do it again in her novel of Sir Walter Raleigh and his times, *The King's Snare*.

Thus do tellers of tales make time timeless and age ageless as they recreate the past in life and love and stirring adventure. But it is not enough to just go back across the years; the learning child must go all over this earth, across all the miles.

> There is no frigate like a book
> To take us miles away.
> —Emily Dickinson

Perhaps one can first begin to appreciate the richness of life that exists wherever many types and cultures build a nation together by coming to know the many cultural groups of the United States. The Indians, of course, were here first. Ann

Nolan Clark's authentic stories grow from her teaching experiences near Santa Fe. In *My Mother's House* is for younger children. *Blue Canyon Horse* relates in singing words a boy's love for his horse, his grief when she returns to the wild herd, and his joy when she returns with her foal. *Little Navajo Bluebird* portrays the emotional conflicts of a Navajo girl as her brother and sister begin to break the closeness of the family when they learn new ways at school. The story of conflict between two generations has significance for all children who are in the midst of such conflict; it is not just another Indian story. These last two will be more enjoyed by ten- or eleven-year-olds.

In *Dancing Cloud*, Mary and Conrad Buff tell the story of the naming of a Navajo boy. It has a haunting sense of the Indian's closeness to nature, to the cycle of life and death. The illustrations are of great beauty.

Eagle Feather by Clyde Bulla is another story of a Navajo Indian boy—his love for his family and hogan and how he finally went to the white man's school. It is a lively tale full of action that small boys like, but emphasizes the strong sense of dignity and independence of the Navajo. The illustrations are by Tom Two Arrows.

For children a little older, Sonia Bleeker is doing a great service in her books describing various tribes. There are seven of them:

The Apache Indians, Raiders of the Southwest
The Cherokee, Indians of the Mountains
The Crow Indians, Hunters of the Northern Plains
The Delaware Indians, Eastern Fishermen and Farmers
Indians of the Longhouse, the Story of the Iroquois
The Sea Hunters, Indians of the Northwest Coast
The Seminole Indians

Margaret Phelps interprets the Southwest Indian in her colorful informative books of that region. *Jaro and the Golden Colt* tells the story of a Hopi boy at the time Coronado's army marched throught Arizona in search of gold and the Seven

Cities of Cibola. Alice Marriott, from long residence in the Southwest and knowledge of the Indians, has told some of their legends in her *Winter-Telling Stories;* she gives a vivid history of the Anasazi, the Ancient Ones of the Southwest, and their descendants, the Pueblos, in *Indians of the Four Corners.* She as vividly interprets the Indians of the Plains in *Indians on Horseback.*

For older children there are many fine stories, both of the Indians of long ago and of the Indians as they are today. In Virginia Voight's *Zeke and the Fisher Cat,* a white boy from Plymouth Colony shares wilderness danger during the Pequot War. In *King Philip,* Esther Averill tells the dramatic story of the last of the Narragansett Chiefs. Zachary Ball tells the story of how Joe Panther, a young Seminole leader, builds good feeling between his people and white people in *Swamp Chief.* In Evelyn Lampman's *Ta-Mah-Na-Wus-Tom* Tom, a Rogue River Indian boy, is caught by hostile tribesmen and sold as a slave. His own skill and courage and friendship with Lieutenant Phil Sheridan change the course of his life.

Another much larger group of people in the United States are the Negroes. Two small boys, one white, one Negro, discover they make a better scooter when they work together in Jerrold Beim's *Two is a Team. My Dog Rinty* by Marie Hall Ets is an original boy and dog story laid in Harlem. For children in the middle grades, Marguerite de Angeli's story of the growing acceptance of the little Negro girl in a Philadelphia girl scout troop is related in *Bright April.* Melindy lived in Chicago. For several generations, some male member of the family had won a medal for bravery. In her generation there was only a girl, but she well deserved the medal she won for her bravery in the big fire. *Melindy's Medal* by Georgene Faulkner tells this story of a brave girl. *Lucky Mischief* by Mebane Burgwyn is a good story of 4-H activities; it also points out excellent values in boys' relationships. For older children *Call Me Charley* by Jesse Jackson, the story of a Negro boy who finds his place in a school where most of the children are white, and *Shuttered Windows* by Florence Crannell Means, the story of a Minnesota Negro girl's conflicts when she goes South for the first time, are fine novels concerned with human relationships. In none of these books are the characters stereotypes; their stories are interesting because they are human beings, not because they are Negroes.

✻ Marguerite de Angeli's exquisite pictures and delightful stories interpret several families and children of other cultures in America: the Amish in *Henner's Lydia*, the Polish in *Up the Hill*, the Swedish in *Elin's America*. Lois Lenski's stories are concerned not so much with cultural groups as with regional groups having particular economic and social problems in such books as *Strawberry Girl* (strawberry pickers in Florida), *Cotton in My Sack* (cotton pickers in Arkansas), *Boom Town Boy* (oil people in Oklahoma).

Florence Crannell Means has written several moving novels for older girls in which each heroine comes from a different cultural group:

Teresita (Spanish)
Shadow Over Wide Ruin (Indian)
The Rains Will Come (Hopi Indian)

It is not often that children like what they call "I books," those written in the first person, and seldom will they accept an "I book" that is really stream of consciousness writing, revealing a child's growth process. *And Now Miguel* by Joseph Krumgold is a notable exception. Miguel belongs to the New Mexican Chavez family of sheep herders. This is the story of his great longing to accompany the men and sheep to their summer pasture in the mountains and his need to be recognized as a maturing individual, told with humor and poignant understanding.

Children may easily find good friends and neighbors from almost every country of the world in colorful books. They enjoy sharing the unique way some children who live in remote places in Canada go to school in Helen Acker's story of *The School Train*. Mary Graham Bonner writes some of the best sports and mystery stories for children in the middle grades. These Canadian boys and girls do not seem very different from United States children in *Out to Win, The Base-Stealer, The Mysterious Caboose, Dugout Mystery,* and several other stories.

Neighbors to the south are delightful to know, whether younger children go to Mexico with Elizabeth Morrow in *The Painted Pig,* to Guatemala with Ann Nolan Clark in *Looking-for-Something,* or to Peru with Helen Parish in *At the Palace Gates.* Those a little older enjoy the Mexican children in Louise Kent Tarshis' *Village that Learned to Read,* Charlie May Simon's *Popo's Miracle,* Delia Goetz' *The Hidden Burro,* or *Magic Money* by Ann Nolan Clark where little Costa Rican Tony finds the answer to his wanting secret about money.

Many Americans feel close to Britain, for her literary heritage is also ours. Every English-speaking child should have the privilege of sharing the reading aloud of Milne's *Winnie the Pooh,* Grahame's *Wind in the Willows,* and Sir James Barrie's *Peter Pan.* Certainly, some children should have the chance to enjoy Lewis Carroll's *Alice in Wonderland,* but they must not be made to feel they are morons if its particular form of fantasy and humor does not appeal to them. Arthur Ransome's stories of the *Swallows and Amazons* and David Severn's *Cruise of the Maiden Castle* or *Treasure for Three* are probably most characteristic of modern writers in England.

Little children will be charmed by the recent, beautiful books from Switzerland, *A Bell for Ursli* and *Florina and the Wild Bird* by Chonz. As they grow a little older, the Buffs' story of the Swiss boy *Kobi* and retelling of the famous William Tell legend in *The Apple and the Arrow* will have great appeal. Probably no European child is as beloved as the little Swiss girl *Heidi,* whose adventures as told by Johanna Spyri probably interpret Swiss life to more children than all textbooks and other books put together. This is almost as true of Kati and Jancsi in Kate Seredy's beautiful vivid recreation of Hungarian farm life in *The Good Master.* Margot Benary-Isbert's courageous family in *The Ark* and *Rowan Farm* are wonderful friends to know as they make a new life for themselves in modern Germany. Their love of animals, their sense of humor, their ability to adapt to almost any circumstance, their appreciation of kindness, their capacity for hard work are universal concerns of all young people, not just German concerns.

Any young person seeking beauty, truth, adventure may enjoy accompanying the three gentlemen seeking these things as they land near Capri and find some answers to their desires as they determine to enter the Blue Grotto in Ann Weil's *Red Sails to Capri.*

There are not yet as many interesting books about children in Africa as there are about Europe and Asia, but children in the middle grades will enjoy the characteristic and lively adventures of the boys in Eleanor Hoffman's *Mischief in Fez* and Norman Davis' *Picken's Great Adventure.*

Sometimes it is a genuine source of wonder as to how it happens that there are so many children's books of distinction about China—pre-communist China, of course. Have our missionaries, teachers, doctors, diplomats, and business agents felt a unique kinship or possibly a respect for Chinese family life which seemed important to share? The Chinese people do not change much despite great political strife. Eleanor Lattimore's *Little Pear* will long be a friend of many eight- and nine-year-olds. Su Mei and her family in Margueritte Bro's *Su Mei's Golden Year,* Young Fu in Elizabeth Lewis' *Young Fu of the Upper Yangtze,* and Li Lun who developed his own special kind of courage, quite different from his father's, in *Li Lun, Lad of Courage* by Carolyn Treffinger are likely to become friends, too.

The whole pattern of village life in Japan is beautifully portrayed in story and picture by Mitsu and Taro Yashima in *The Village Tree. Crow Boy,* also by Yashima, is a wonderful portrait of a slow-learning boy in a Japanese school; it is poignant and of universal appeal. These Japanese children have the observant curiosity, the friendliness, and the happiness of children the world over. Add to this *The Forbidden Forest* by Darrell Berrigan and John Dominis with its beautiful photographs, and children will almost feel they have been in Japan. Pearl Buck takes children to Japan in *The Big Wave* and to the China she knew so well in *The Water Buffalo Children, The Chinese Children Next Door,* and *Yu Lan: Flying Boy of China.*

Young children also feel close to the children of India in the Loudens' story with the beautiful pictures, *Rain in the Winds,* or in de Golish's story of *Mamba-Kan,* a baby elephant and his friendship with a little Indian boy, Velu. This story also is accompanied by wonderful photographs. Jean Bothwell, who lived in India many years, has several exciting stories of Indian children for older readers: *Little Boat Boy, The Thirteenth Stone, River Boy of Kashmir, Star of India.* And who can place the singing prose of the jungle, animals, and children of Rudyard Kipling in his *Just-So Stories, Jungle Books,* and *Kim?* Their locale is India, but their place is the world. They truly belong to all children everywhere. Some stories seem written to be read aloud, for example, the inimitable Just-So Stories, "Oh, best beloved." Maybe some reading child who has also been read to will pass on his rich heritage by reading to young friends; this factor, by the way, is a better motivation for reading than we often recognize.

Bruce was once told in school that they were going to study foreign children. Coming home, he asked his mother who and what "furn" children were. She explained that they were children who lived in other lands, who spoke a little differently from the way we did, who also ate different food and wore different clothes.

"But are they just children like we are?"

"Yes, dear," patiently answered his mother.

"Well," he said with considerable vigor, "if they are just children, I wouldn't think you'd have to study them to know them."

Children round the world are friends in books, friends in reality.

Our Heritage of Folk Tales, Poetry, and Music

Surely one of the best keys to knowledge of any people anywhere is through understanding of their needs and desires in music, art, and literature. Myths and legends often embody a people's best efforts to tell of their origin, gods, and heroes. Folk tales stem from the people and are truly a sort of distilled essence of people's ways of living, love of beauty, sense of humor, values, and ideals.

The folk tale, whether about man or animal, often possesses wisdom and has basic humor and interesting adventure. Those about human beings frequently had their origin in a true story of someone's outstanding achievement or deeds, in some work or activity characteristic of the region from which it comes. Someone comes along with more imagination than the original teller of the tale, and says, "Well, if he was that good, I can make him better." By the time this has happened many times, the mixture of reality and imagination has grown beyond recognition. The hero conquers the limitations of his way of life by cleverness or extra power in which there may also be an element of magic or of the supernatural. The word magic is rather out of favor in this scientific age, but it is interesting to notice that at present one of the most popular forms of description of almost anything which delights one beyond ordinary enjoyment is, "It's out of this world." After all, any scientific experiment involves all the knowledge one has, all the techniques one knows how to use, and something more. No one knows just what will happen; but something *new* occurs. It's magic; it's "out of this world." Actually, that hopeful, daring, adventurous element in life makes the adventurer, experimenter, explorer, or discoverer—child or man—revel in the "magic," the unpredictable, the unknown element. Of course, the next generation will explain it in scientific terms, but the cow and Pecos Bill's Slewfoot Sue still go over the moon. There is always new, inexplicable magic to egg one on. Thus, the folk hero becomes an extension of ourselves, and the child or adult enters all experience, including some "out of this world," by thrilling indentification with him. The folk hero becomes one of the most alluring characters to know. Years ago, one could know these stories of one's own people or those nearby only as handed down by word of mouth. Not today. Stories of peoples all over the earth are written down and put into books, because man now knows how to communicate through the written word.

As the folk tale is told to generation after generation, it becomes disciplined in form. Extraneous concepts and useless words are chiseled away so that each part remaining is essential to the whole. It is like a cut stone, each facet of which reflects part of the whole beauty. Thus, there is design and form in the folk tale, often far beyond that of any other literary medium except poetry. It is, of course, close to folk music and dance, so that frequently songs and dances express the same feelings and ideas that have evolved in the folk tale. The common music and art form, A B A—an introduction, a theme developed by exposition, contrast and repetition, a conclusion or coda—is a common form of the folk tale. By means of this folk tale, the creation of many people becomes a human ladder to better understanding, a kind of spiritual bridge on which we may walk across to each other. All too frequently, we lose sight of this human value in our emphasis upon the literary form or significance of the folk tale, myth, or legend. Perhaps children can help restore this human value.

American folk tales grow and grow. They are of the American spirit, different from the folk tales with the individual characteristics of the English, Dutch, Spanish, French and Germans who first came to this country. The pioneer clearing forests evolved a giant lumber man, Paul Bunyan; the cowboy taming wild horses evolved a super cowboy, Pecos Bill; the builders of transcontinental railroads evolved a super-engineer, Casey Jones, and hammer-driving giant, John Henry; the sailor along the sea-coast evolved a super-whaling giant, Old Stormalong.

These people worked hard and used the resources at hand to meet every need. That is essentially American, and we feel close to these folk heroes of ours. We laugh *with* them, not *at* them, for their humor is our particular American kind. Even hardy pioneer adventurers like Davy Crockett, Daniel Boone, and Johnny Appleseed grew into folk heroes so that what we know of them today is part legend, part history.

In this country's growing, people from Europe and Africa went into certain sections of the country, bringing with them their music, their tales, their art, their customs, and their ways of living. Sometimes they had little contact with the outside world, so there is preserved a body of folk lore of their own, little influenced by life in the rest of America. In the Appalachian and Cumberland mountains are English tales of long ago such as the Jack tales, often still told with old English accent and words; in parts of Pennsylvania are German art and folkways we call Pennsylvania Dutch; in the deep south the Negro stories stem from African tales (Br'er Rabbit may have hopped across the Atlantic once upon a time); in Louisiana there is a French flavor to stories as well as food in the Bayou country; in California and the Southwest, there is a Spanish rhythm in song and story. American folk lore and folk music have been influenced by the folk arts from many cultures.

The typical American folk hero is a hard-working, fun-loving giant who faces and conquers his world and is still growing. His words and his songs are ours, for the development of the folk tale and the folk song is never finished. They are our heritage and part of our growing experience. We enter the stream of life and grow, too, whether we whip our weight in wildcats as Davy Crockett or conquer space as Superman. We sing "On Top of Old Smoky" and "Casey Jones," both out of our past; but we also sing the contemporary "On Mockingbird Hill" and "Shrimp Boats Are A-Coming." The folk tale and the folk song are of the stream of life.

There are not many retellings for very young children, since this interest develops more after the age of nine or thereabouts. No one, however, should miss *Journey Cake, Ho!*, Ruth Sawyer's delightful version of the possible origin of Johnnycake written with true folk flavor. The hilarious illustrations by Robert McCloskey add much to the story.

American literature has made its own versions of English folklore, such as *The Three Little Pigs;* of Scandinavian tales, such as *The Three Billy Goats Gruff;* and of German tales, such as *The Musicians of Bremen* or *Hansel and Gretel.* These tales are available in many collections. Many of the German tales were retold by the Grimm brothers in their *Household Tales* of which there are many fine editions.

There are several good anthologies of American folk tales worth owning. Carl Carmer includes songs and some of the best versions of beloved tall tales from the North, South, East, and West in *America Sings.* The striking pictures by his wife, Elizabeth Carmer, add much to the enjoyment of the book. Anne Malcolmson's *Yankee Doodle's Cousins* is also a good collection. *American Folklore* by Botkin, is not for children's reading but is an excellent source book for the teacher or parent with a genuine interest in folklore.

Ol' Paul by Glen Rounds is a vigorous version of the Paul Bunyan tales, the format of which—including the selection of type, paper, and binding—is singularly appropriate to the story. Harold Felton's *Paul Bunyan Legends* is strikingly illustrated by Richard Bennett. Esther Shephard's *Paul Bunyan* has excellent illustrations by Rockwell Kent.

Probably the best retelling of the Pecos Bill tales with which to begin is *Pecos Bill and Lightning* by Leigh Peck. Other lively retellings are by Harold Felton in *Pecos Bill: Texas Cowpuncher* and by James Bowman in *Pecos Bill, the Greatest Cowboy of All Time.*

Richard Chase is one of our best collectors of tales from the eastern mountains, especially of Jack Tales. These are in two collections: *Jack Tales* and *Grandfather Tales.* Two of the very best are published in individual volumes, *Jack and the Three Sillies* and *Wicked John and the Devil.*

Irwin Shapiro has a rare gift for drama and humor in his versions of some of our best tall tales. The brief, swiftly-paced text and the almost cartoonlike illustrations make these of special interest to many slow readers, although they will also be enjoyed by every reader:

Casey Jones and Locomotive No. 638
How Old Stormalong Captured the Mocha Dick
John Henry and the Double Jointed Steam Drill
Steamboat Bill and the Captain's Top Hat

The tales that Meridel Le Seuer writes should be read aloud for their ringing, swinging rhythm and the wonderful sound of the words. *Little Brother of the Wilderness* is the story of Johnny Appleseed, who planted apple orchards all through Ohio and Indiana; *Chanticleer of Wilderness Road* is the tale of "tall talkin', tall walkin' " Davy Crockett.

But it is not only the American folk tale that finds its way into print today. Folk tales from many lands are beautifully retold and are good to read aloud or by oneself. From China, there are two charming collections by Lim Sian-tek, *Folk Tales from China* and *More Folk Tales from China.* From Japan comes Uchida's *The Dancing Kettle and Other Japanese Folk Tales.* From Africa there is the group of folk tales about small deer and other animals, *Kantchil's Lime Pit,* and the African tales *Cowtail Switch and Other Stories,* both collected by Harold Courlander. The Robert Kane illustrations in *Kantchil's Lime Pit* are unique and give a special flavor to the stories.

Mary Hatch tells sparkling tales of humor from Denmark in *Thirteen Danish Tales;* Roger Duvoisin portrays a vigorous, humorous group from Switzerland in *Three Sneezes and Other Swiss Tales;* Robert Davis writes about the gentlemanly Spanish pig *Padre Porko;* Alice Kelsey depicts the merry Turkish simpleton who somehow always manages to come out on top in *Once the Hodja;* James Bowman tells colorful, droll stories from

Finland in *Tales from a Finnish Tupa;* Charles Finger relates exciting South American tales in *Tales from Silver Lands;* and Frank Henius retells tales in *Stories from the Americas.* Many of the best-loved tales from all over the world provide fun, adventure, and, once in a while, even a moral or two for their readers. Many are excellent for dramatization.

The great Norse and Greek myths are a literary heritage, so woven into the background of our culture that they should be an essential part of every child's experience, whether listened to or read by himself. Good beginnings may be made with Dorothy Hosford's *Thunder of the Gods, By His Own Might* (Beowulf) and Catherine F. Sellew's *Adventures with the Giants* and *Adventures with the Heroes.* Perhaps no versions are so wonderful to read aloud as those in the beautiful rhythmic prose of Padraic Colum:

Children of Odin
Children's Homer
The Golden Fleece and Heroes before Achilles

Sally Benson retells Greek and Roman myths from Bulfinch's *Age of Fable* in one of the most readable editions for children, *Stories of the Gods and Heroes.* For mature readers, Olivia Coolidge tells Norse and Greek myths in stirring prose: *Legends of the North, Greek Myths, The Trojan War.*

Not only in folk tales, myths and legends, but also in fables such as those of Aesop and La Fontaine do children discover that all through the ages men have taught children lessons and values by means of stories.

Aesop's Fables
Fables of La Fontaine (translated by Margaret Wise Brown)

Another rich source of history and story is in ballads to be read aloud in groups or by oneself, to be sung, to be dramatized. Anne Malcolmson provides the ballad and Virginia Lee Burton illustrations, fascinating both in design and in the exquisite detail of drawing, for the Song of Robin Hood.

Elinor Parker's *100 Story Poems* and *100 Poems about People,* Louis Untermeyer's *The Magic Circle* and Tobbitt and White's two collections, *Dramatized Ballads* and *The Saucy Sailor and Other Dramatized Ballads,* offer a wide choice for rhythmic narrative. There is nothing quite like a singing story. This list is not complete by any means, but these choices are among the good versions with which to live. They can lead the reader to many others.

It is almost impossible to write about folklore and ballads without also mentioning folk music, although that deserves another book for itself. Every family should have a few good collections such as Ruth Seeger's *American Folk Songs for Children* and *American Animal Songs for Children;* Boni and Lloyd's *Fireside Book of Folk Songs* and *Fireside Book of American Folk Songs.* This folk heritage in story and song opens wide the doors to understanding this earth and the people who made and are making our world, from the earliest times on down through the great march of history. Adventure, beauty, humor—here is the stuff of life to which is added the priceless gift of imagination.

For Children to Age 9

Stories

The School Train	Helen Acker	Abelard-Schuman
Three Little Steps	Charlotte Beeker	Scribner
Three Little Steps and the Party		Scribner
Three Little Steps and the Snow Dog		Scribner
Three Little Steps and the Spotted Horse		Scribner
Kid Brother	Jerrold Beim	Morrow
Tim and the Tool Chest		Morrow
Two Is a Team		Harcourt, Brace
Country Store		Morrow
Country Garage		Morrow

Bill and His Neighbors	Ruth Benedict and Gene Weltfish	Houghton-Mifflin
Races and People	Boyd and Asimov	Abelard-Schuman
The Noon Balloon	Margaret W. Brown	Scott
Here Comes the School Train	William Bunce	Dutton
The Lucky Baseball Bat	Matthew F. Christopher	Little, Brown
In My Mother's House	Ann Nolan Clark	Viking
Danny's Luck	Lavinia Davis	Doubleday
Roger and the Fox		Doubleday
Wild Birthday Cake		Doubleday
The School Bus Picnic	Aaron Fine	Holt
Terry and Bunky Play Baseball	Dick Fishel	Putnam
Terry and Bunky Play Basketball		Putnam
Terry and Bunky Play Football		Putnam
Lunch Box Story	Maia Goldberg	Holiday House
Mei Li	Thomas Handforth	Doubleday
B Is for Betsy	Carolyn B. Haywood	Harcourt, Brace
Back to School with Betsy		Harcourt, Brace
Two and Two Are Four		Harcourt, Brace
Nappy Wanted a Friend	Inez Hogan	Dutton
Willy's Farm	Edith Hurd and Clement	Lothrop, Lee & Shepard
Spring Comes to Meadowbrook Farm	Katherine Keelor	Nelson
Summer Comes to Meadowbrook Farm		Nelson
Autumn Comes to Meadowbrook Farm		Nelson
Winter Comes to Meadowbrook Farm		Nelson
First Grade	Eleanor Lattimore	Morrow
Tommy and Dee Dee	Yen Liang	Oxford
Red Light, Green Light	Golden MacDonald	Doubleday
Blueberries for Sal	Robert McCloskey	Viking

One Morning in Maine		Viking
Make Way for Ducklings		Viking
All around the Town	Phyllis Maginley	Lippincott
Store at Criss Cross Corners	Marjorie Medary	Abingdon
Krista and the Frosty Packages	Helen Olds	Messner
Big City	Maud and Miska Petersham	Macmillan
Little Town		Macmillan
Juanita	Leo Politi	Scribner
Heart for Baseball	Marion Renick	Scribner
Jimmy's Own Basketball		Scribner
Nicky's Football Team		Scribner
Peter's Home Run		Scribner
Market Day for Ti Andre	Maia Rodman	Viking
While Susie Sleeps	Nina Schneider	Doubleday
Follow the Sunset	Nina and Herman Schneider	Doubleday
Lucky Days for Johnny	Irene Smith	Whittlesey House
Tim and the Brass Buttons	Ruth Tooze	Messner
Wires Up!		Messner

For Children Age 9-15

Nonfiction with a New Look

The Pony Express	Samuel H. Adams	Random House
America before Man	Elizabeth C. Baity	Viking
Americans before Columbus		Viking
Land of William of Orange	Adrian Barnouw	Lippincott
Communication from Cave Man to Television	Julie F. Batchelor	Harcourt, Brace
Workshops for the World	Graham Beckel	Abelard-Schuman
Germany	Elsa R. Berner	Holiday House
The Apache Indians, Raiders of the Southwest	Sonia Bleeker	Morrow
The Cherokee Indians of the Mountains		Morrow

The Chippewa Indians, Rice Gatherers of the Great Lakes		Morrow
The Crow Indians, Hunters of the Northern Plains		Morrow
The Delaware Indians, Eastern Fishermen and Farmers		Morrow
Indians of the Longhouse: The Story of the Iriquois		Morrow
The Pueblo Indians, Farmers of the Rio Grande		Morrow
The Sea Hunters, Indians of the Northwest Coast		Morrow
The Seminole Indians		Morrow
Oceania	Charles Borden	Holiday House
Land of William Tell	Lillian Bragdon	Lippincott
Land of Joan of Arc		Lippincott
Arab Lands	Mary Brittain	Holiday House
Land and People of Brazil	Rose Brown	Lippincott
A World Full of Homes	William A. Burns	Whittlesey House
Australia	Rafaello Busoni	Holiday House
Italy		Holiday House
Mexico		Holiday House
America Begins	Alice Dalgliesh	Scribner
America Builds Homes	Dalgliesh and Maloy	Scribner
Wooden Shoes		Scribner
Landing of the Pilgrims	James Daugherty	Random House
France	Robert Davis	Holiday House
Picture Story of Holland	Dola De Jong	McKay
Dutch East Indies	Cateau De Leeuw	Holiday House
Big Family of Peoples	Irmengarde Eberle	Crowell
Turkey Old and New	Selma Ekrem	Scribner
We Are the Government	Mary Elting	Doubleday
First Book of Mexico	Sam and Beryl Epstein	Watts
Scandinavia	Edwin Ben Evans	Holiday House
All about Us	Eva Knox Evans	Capitol

People Are Important		Capitol
Why We Live Where We Live		Little, Brown
The Land We Live On	Carroll L. and Mildred A. Fenton	Doubleday
Our Independence and the Constitution	Dorothy C. Fisher	Random House
A Fair World for All: The Meaning of the Declaration of Human Rights		Whittlesey House
The Barbary Pirates	C. F. Forester	Random House
Augustus Caesar's World	Genevieve Foster	Scribner
George Washington's World		Scribner
Abraham Lincoln's World		Scribner
How the United Nations Works	Tom Galt	Crowell
Here Is Africa	Attilio Gatti	Scribner
Here Is the Veldt		Scribner
Land and People of Greece	T. Gianapoulis	Lippincott
Mediterranean Spotlights		Scribner
Picture Story of China	Emily Hahn	McKay
First Book of India		Watts
Land and People of Israel	Gail Hoffman	Lippincott
Capitol Hill	Desider Holisher	Abelard-Schuman
Picture Story of France	Clarke Hutton	Watts
Turkey	Vernon Ives	Holiday House
The Vikings	Elizabeth Janeway	Random House
Clipper Ship Days	John Jennings	Random House
Lee and Grant at Appomattox	McKinley Kantor	Random House
Land of the Polish People	Eric Kelly	Lippincott
Here Is India	Jean Kennedy	Scribner
Brazil	Leonard Kenworthy	Random House
Yugoslavia	George Kish	Holiday House
Your America	Kohl and Nisenson	World
First Book of Israel	Nora B. Kubie	Watts

Genghis Khan	Harold Lamb	Random House
Land and People of Mexico	Elsa Larralda	Lippincott
Four Ways of Being Human	Gene Litsitzky	Viking
Vast Horizons	Mary S. Lucas	Viking
Our Country, America	Chrystie McFall	Macmillan
The Mexican Story	May McNeer and Lynd Ward	Farrar, Straus, & Cudahy
Land and People of Sweden	Frederic C. Mano	Lippincott
The Growing Human Family	Minoo Masani	Oxford
Winter at Valley Forge	Van Wyck Mason	Random House
First Book of Japan	Helen Mears	Watts
Land and People of India	Manorama Modak	Lippincott
Land of the Russian People	Alexander Nazaroff	Lippincott
Lewis and Clark Expedition	Richard Neuberger	Random House
Land and People of Ireland	Elinor O'Brien	Lippincott
Picture Story of Sweden	Hester O'Neill	McKay
Picture Story of Hawaii		McKay
Land and People of South Africa	Alan Paton	Lippincott
Little Geography of the United States	Mabel Pyne	Houghton Mifflin
Little History of the United States		Houghton Mifflin
Picture Map Geography of Asia	Vernon Quinn	Lippincott
Picture Map Geography of South America		Lippincott
Picture Map Geography of Mexico, Central America and West Indies		Lippincott
Picture Map Geography of the United States		Lippincott

Picture Map Geography of Alaska and Canada		Lippincott
Picture Map Geography of Africa		Lippincott
Pageant of the Seven Seas		Lippincott
Commemorative Stamps of the U.S.A.	Fred Reinfeld	Crowell
Custer's Last Stand	Quentin Reynolds	Random House
Battle of Britain		Random House
Partners: The United Nations and Youth	Eleanor Roosevelt and Helen Ferris	Doubleday
Land and People of Canada	Frances Ross	Lippincott
New Found World	Katherine Shippen	Viking
Great Heritage		Viking
I Know a City		Viking
Passage to America		Harper
The Pool of Knowledge		Harper
British Isles	William Sloane	Holiday House
Japan	Cornelia Spencer	Holiday House
Low Countries		Holiday House
Land of the Chinese People		Lippincott
Voyages of Christopher Columbus	Armstrong Sperry	Random House
Here Is Alaska	Evelyn Stefansson	Scribner
United Nations: New York	Dorothy Sterling	Doubleday
Land of the English People	Alicia Street	Lippincott
The Louisiana Purchase	Robert Tallant	Random House
Egypt	Alice Taylor	Holiday House
Getting to Know Korea	Regina Tor	Coward
Getting to Know Germany		Coward
Getting to Know Puerto Rico		Coward
Land and People of Japan	Josephine Vaughan	Lippincott

Windows for the Crown Prince	Elizabeth G. Vining	Lippincott
Put Democracy to Work	Ruth H. Wagner	Abelard-Schuman
Adventures and Discoveries of Marco Polo	Richard Walsh	Random House
The Crusades	Anthony West	Random House
Prehistoric America	Anne Terry White	Random House
Queen Elizabeth and the Spanish Armada	Frances Winwar	Random House
Land and People of Italy		Lippincott

Biography

Daniel Boone	Esther Averill	Harper
First Woman Doctor: Elizabeth Blackwell	Nina Baker	Messner
George Washington: First President	Elsie Ball	Abingdon
Sigmund Freud	Ivy Bolton	Messner
Father Junipero Serra		Messner
George Washington Carver	Arna Bontemps	Random House
Daniel Boone	John Mason Brown	Random House
The Man Who Changed China: Story of Sun Yat-sen	Pearl Buck	Random House
Richard Wagner, Who Followed a Star	Gladys Burch	Holt
Kit Carson	Edmund Collier	Random House
Young Hans Christian Andersen	Hedwig Collin	Viking
America's Robert E. Lee	Henry S. Commager	Houghton Mifflin
Ben Franklin of Old Philadelphia	Margaret Cousins	Random House
Abraham Lincoln	James Daugherty	Viking
Daniel Boone		Viking
Poor Richard		Viking
Marcus and Narcissa Whitman		Viking
Of Courage Undaunted (Lewis and Clark)		Viking

Leif the Lucky	Ingri and Edgar d'Aulaire	Doubleday
George Washington		Doubleday
Abraham Lincoln		Doubleday
Benjamin Franklin		Doubleday
Pocahontas		Doubleday
Christopher Columbus		Doubleday
Edvard Grieg	Sybil Deucher	Dutton
The Young Brahms		Dutton
Walt Whitman	Babette Deutsch	Messner
Washington, the Nation's First Hero	Jeanette Eaton	Morrow
Lee, the Gallant General		Morrow
George Gershwin	David Ewen	Holt
Haydn: A Good Life		Holt
Winged Moccasins: Story of Sacajawea	Frances Farnsworth	Messner
America's Paul Revere	Esther Forbes	Houghton Mifflin
George Washington	Genevieve Foster	Scribner
Andrew Jackson		Scribner
Abraham Lincoln		Scribner
Theodore Roosevelt		Scribner
Chief Joseph of the Nez Perces	Shannon Garst	Messner
Jack London		Messner
Albert Schweitzer	Joseph Gollomb	Vanguard
Deep Flowing Brook (Bach)	Madeleine Goss	Holt
Unfinished Symphony (Schubert)		Holt
Beethoven, Master Musician		Holt
Brahms, the Master	Goss and Schauffler	Holt
Christopher Columbus, Discoverer	Alberta P. Graham	Abingdon
Lafayette, Friend of America		Abingdon
La Salle, River Explorer		Abingdon
Your Most Humble Servant, Benjamin Banneker	Shirley Graham	Messner

George Washington Carver		Messner
Mary McLeod Bethune		Messner
The Wright Brothers	Haines and Morrill	Abingdon
William Penn, Founder and Friend	Virginia Haviland	Abingdon
We Grew Up in America	Alice Hazeltine	Abingdon
America's Ethan Allen	Stewart Holbrook	Houghton Mifflin
Wild Bill Hickok Tames the West		Random House
George Washington	Clara I. Judson	Follett
Thomas Jefferson		Follett
Andrew Jackson		Follett
Abraham Lincoln		Follett
Theodore Roosevelt		Follett
John James Audubon	John and M. Keiran	Random House
Twelve Citizens of the World	Leonard Kenworthy	Doubleday
Louis Braille	J. Kugelmass	Messner
Ralph J. Bunche		Messner
Florence Nightingale	Margaret Leighton	Grosset & Dunlap
Albert Einstein	Elma E. Levinger	Messner
John Philip Sousa	Anna Lingg	Holt
Mozart, Genius of Harmony		Holt
Mephisto Waltz: Franz Liszt		Holt
Story of Albert Schweitzer	Jo Manton	Abelard-Schuman
Dolly Madison	Jane Mayer	Random House
Story of Davy Crockett	Enid Meadowcroft	Grosset & Dunlap
Story of Crazy Horse		Grosset & Dunlap
Story of Martha Washington	Jeanette Nolan	Grosset & Dunlap
On Our Way	Robert Patterson	Holiday House
Stephen Foster	Catherine Peare	Holt

John James Audubon		Holt
Henry Wadsworth Longfellow		Holt
Louisa May Alcott		Holt
Mark Twain		Holt
Robert Louis Stevenson		Holt
Albert Einstein		Holt
Marco Polo	Olive Price	Grosset & Dunlap
He Heard America Sing: Stephen Foster	Claire Lee Purdy	Messner
Song of the North: Grieg		Messner
Anton Dvorak		Messner
The Wright Brothers	Quentin Reynolds	Random House
Leonardo da Vinci	Elizabeth Ripley	Oxford
Michelangelo		Oxford
Van Gogh		Oxford
Rembrandt		Oxford
The Jim Thorpe Story	Gene Schoor	Messner
The Red Grange Story		Messner
Thomas Jefferson, Father of Democracy	Vincent Sheehan	Random House
Moses	Katherine Shippen	Harper
Leif Erikson		Harper
Michael Faraday: From Errand Boy to Master Physicist	Harry Sootin	Messner
John Paul Jones	Armstrong Sperry	Random House
Story of Daniel Boone	William O. Steele	Grosset & Dunlap
Elizabeth Tudor	Marguerite Vance	Dutton
Lady Jane Grey		Dutton
Martha, Daughter of Virginia		Dutton
Marie Antoinette, Daughter of an Empire		Dutton
On Wings of Fire: Rose Hawthorne		Dutton
Story of Robert E. Lee	Iris Vinton	Grosset & Dunlap

Leif Ericson, Explorer	Ruth Cromer Weir	Abingdon
Thomas Alva Edison, Inventor		Abingdon
Handel at the Court of Kings	Opal Wheeler	Dutton
Ludwig Beethoven and the Chiming Tower Bells		Dutton
Stephen Foster and His Little Dog Tray		Dutton
Frederic Chopin: Early Years		Dutton
Frederic Chopin: Later Years		Dutton
Paganini, Master of Strings		Dutton
Story of Peter Tschaikovsky: Part I		Dutton
Hans Andersen, Son of Denmark		Dutton
Mozart, the Wonder Boy	Wheeler and Deucher	Dutton
Joseph Haydn, the Merry Little Peasant		Dutton
Sebastian Bach, Boy of Thuringia		Dutton
Franz Schubert and His Merry Friends		Dutton
Edward MacDowell and His Cabin in the Pines		Dutton
Millet Tilled the Soil		Dutton
Giotto Tended the Sheep		Dutton
My Brother Was Mozart	Wheeler and Purdy	Holt
Napoleon and the Battle of Waterloo	Frances Winwar	Random House
Walter Reed	L. N. Wood	Messner
Lonely Crusader: Life of Florence Nightingale	Cecil Woodham-Smith	Whittlesey House
Sam Houston, Fighter and Leader	Frances Wright	Abingdon

Fiction with Historical Background, and That of Other Cultures

King Philip	Esther Averill	Harper
Swamp Chief	Zachary Ball	Holiday House
The First Thanksgiving	Lena Barksdale	Knopf

The Wonderful Year	Nancy Barnes	Messner
Peter and Wendy	Sir James Barrie	Scribner
Two Is a Team	Jerrold Beim	Harcourt, Brace
The Ark	Benary-Isbert	Harcourt, Brace
Out to Win	Mary Bonner	Knopf
The Base Stealer		Knopf
Dugout Mystery		Knopf
Mystery of the Caboose		Knopf
Little Boat Boy	Jean Bothwell	Harcourt, Brace
The Thirteenth Stone		Harcourt, Brace
River Boy of Kashmir		Morrow
Star of India		Morrow
Su Mei's Golden Year	Margueritte Bro	Doubleday
The Big Wave	Pearl Buck	John Day
The Water Buffalo Children		John Day
The Chinese Children Next Door		John Day
Yu Lan: Flying Boy of China		John Day
Dancing Cloud	Mary and Conrad Buff	Viking
Kobi		Viking
The Apple and the Arrow		Houghton Mifflin
Eagle Feather	Clyde Bulla	Crowell
Lucky Mischief	Mebane Burgwyn	Oxford
A Flag for the Fort	Carl Carmer	Messner
Children of the Covered Wagon	Mary Jane Carr	Crowell
Alice in Wonderland	Lewis Carroll	Grosset & Dunlap
Tree of Freedom	Rebecca Caudill	Viking
A Bell for Ursli	Selina Chonz	Oxford
Florina and the Wild Bird		Oxford
The Wonderful Winter	Marchette Chute	Dutton
Introduction to Shakespeare		Dutton
In My Mother's House	Ann Nolan Clark	Viking
Blue Canyon Horse		Viking
Little Navajo Bluebird		Viking
Looking-For-Something		Viking

Magic Money		Viking
The First Adventure	Elizabeth Coatsworth	Macmillan
The Wishing Pear		Macmillan
Boston Bells		Macmillan
Aunt Flora		Macmillan
Old Whirlwind		Macmillan
The Sod House		Macmillan
The Thanksgiving Story	Alice Dalgliesh	Scribner
Picken's Great Adventure	Norman Davis	Oxford
Door in the Wall	Marguerite De Angeli	Doubleday
Bright April		Doubleday
Elin's America		Doubleday
Henner's Lydia		Doubleday
Up the Hill		Doubleday
Mamba-Kan	Vitold de Golish	John Day
My Dog Rinty	Marie Hall Ets	Viking
Su Won and Her Wonderful Tree	Virginia Fairfax	Dutton
Melindy's Medal	Georgene Faulkner	Messner
Johnny Tremaine	Esther Forbes	Houghton Mifflin
The Hidden Burro	Delia Goetz	Morrow
Wind in the Willows	Kenneth Grahame	Scribner
Adam of the Road	Elizabeth J. Gray	Viking
Johnny Texas	Carol Hoff	Follett
Johnny Texas on the San Antonio Road		Follett
Mischief in Fez	Eleanor Hoffman	Holiday
The Gabriel Horn	Felix Holt	Dutton
Call Me Charley	Jesse Jackson	Harper
Hidden Treasure of Glaston	Eleanore Jewett	Viking
Boy of the Pyramids	Ruth Fosdick Jones	Random House
Rebel Siege	Jim Kielgard	Holiday House
Just So Stories	Rudyard Kipling	Doubleday
The Jungle Book: Books I and II		Doubleday
Kim		Doubleday
And Now Miguel	Joseph Krumgold	Crowell
Bounces of Cynthiann	Evelyn Lampman	Doubleday

Tree Wagon		Doubleday
Ta-Mah-Na-Wus-Tom		Doubleday
Young Fu of the Upper Yangtse	Eleanor Lewis	Winston
Witch of Merthyn	Richard Llewellyn	Doubleday
The Golden Conquest	Helen Lobdell	Little, Brown
The King's Snare		Little, Brown
Rain in the Winds	George and Claire Louden	Scribner
Kim Rides the Tiger	Evelyn McCune	John Day
Moccasin Trail	Eloise McGraw	Coward
Mara: Daughter of the Nile		Coward
Indians of Four Corners	Alice Marriott	Crowell
Indians on Horseback		Crowell
Susanna, the Pioneer Cow	Miriam Mason	Macmillan
Sugarbush Family		Macmillan
The Middle Sister		Macmillan
Ship Boy with Columbus	Enid Meadowcroft	Crowell
The First Year		Crowell
Silver for General Washington		Crowell
By Wagon and Flatboat		Crowell
By Secret Railway		Crowell
On Indian Trails with Daniel Boone		Crowell
Texas Star		Crowell
Shuttered Windows	Florence C. Means	Houghton Mifflin
Teresita		Houghton Mifflin
Shadow over Wide Ruin		Houghton Mifflin
The Rains Will Come		Houghton Mifflin
A Cheese for Lafayette	Elizabeth Meg	Putnam
Candle in the Sky	Elizabeth Meigs	Dutton
Winnie the Pooh	A. A. Milne	Dutton
The Painted Pig	Elizabeth Morrow	Knopf
At the Palace Gates	Helen Rand Parish	Viking
Jaro and the Golden Colt	Margaret Phelps	Macrae Smith
Swallows and Amazons	Arthur Ransome	Lippincott

The Good Master	Kate Seredy	Viking
Cruise of the Maiden Castle	David Severn	Macmillan
Treasure for Three		Macmillan
Popo's Miracle	Charlie May Simon	Dutton
Heidi	Johanna Spyri	Grossett & Dunlap
The Village That Learned to Read	Elizabeth Tarshis	Houghton Mifflin
Li Lun, Lad of Courage	Caroline Treffinger	Abingdon
Zeke and the Fisher Cat	Virginia F. Voight	Holiday
Highland Rebel	Sally Watson	Holt
Red Sails to Capri	Ann Weil	Viking
Will Shakespeare and the Globe Theatre	Anne Terry White	Random House
Little House in the Big Woods	Laura Ingalls Wilder	Harper
Little House on the Prairie		Harper
On the Banks of Plum Creek		Harper
These Happy Golden Years		Harper
The Village Tree	Taro Yashima	Viking
Plenty to Watch		Viking
Crow Boy		Viking

Folk Tales, Poetry, and Music

Fables	Aesop	Garden City
Stories of the Gods and Heroes	Sally Benson	Pantheon
Fireside Book of Folk Songs	Boni and Loyd	Simon & Schuster
Fireside Book of American Folk Songs		Simon & Schuster
American Folklore	Benjamin Botkin	Coward
Pecos Bill, the Greatest Cowboy of Them All	James C. Bowman	Whitman
Tales from a Finnish Tupa		Whitman
Age of Fable	Thomas Bulfinch	Garden City
America Sings	Carl Carmer	Knopf
Jack Tales	Richard Chase	Houghton Mifflin
Grandfather Tales		Houghton Mifflin

Jack and the Three Sillies		Houghton Mifflin
Wicked John and the Devil		Houghton Mifflin
Children of Odin	Padraic Colum	Macmillan
Children's Homer		Macmillan
Golden Fleece and Heroes before Achilles		Macmillan
Legends of the North	Olivia Coolidge	Houghton Mifflin
Greek Myths		Houghton Mifflin
The Trojan War		Houghton Mifflin
Kantchil's Lime Pit	Harold Courlander	Harcourt, Brace
Cowtail Switch and Other Stories		Holt
The Three Sneezes and Other Swiss Tales	Roger Duvoisin	Knopf
Paul Bunyan Legends	Howard W. Felton	Knopf
Pecos Bill		Knopf
Tales from Silver Lands	Charles Finger	Doubleday
Tales from Grimm (illustrated by Wanda Gag)	Grimm Brothers	Coward
Grimm's Fairy Tales		Grosset & Dunlap
Household Tales from Grimm		Macmillan
Thirteen Danish Tales	Mary C. Hatch	Harcourt, Brace
More Danish Tales		Harcourt, Brace
Stories from the Americas	Frank Henius	Scribner
Thunder of the Gods	Dorothy Hosford	Holt
By His Own Might (Beowulf)		Holt
Once the Hodja	Alice G. Kelsey	Longmans, Green
Fables from La Fontaine (17 translated by Margaret Wise Brown)	Jean de La Fontaine	Harper
Folk Tales from China	Sian-tek Lim	John Day

More Folk Tales from China		John Day
Yankee Doodle's Cousins	Anne Malcolmson	Houghton Mifflin
Song of Robin Hood		Houghton Mifflin
100 Story Poems	Elinor Parker	Crowell
100 Poems about People		Crowell
Pecos Bill and Lightning	Leigh Peck	Houghton Mifflin
Ol' Paul	Glen Rounds	Holiday House
Journey Cake, Ho!	Ruth Sawyer	Viking
American Folk Songs for Children	Ruth Seeger	Doubleday
Animal Folk Songs for Children		Doubleday
Adventure with the Giants	Catherine F. Sellew	Little, Brown
Adventure with the Heroes		Little, Brown
How Old Stormalong Captured the Mocha Dick	Irwin Shapiro	Messner
Casey Jones and Locomotive No. 638		Messner
John Henry and His Double-Jointed Steam Drill		Messner
Steamboat Bill and the Captain's Top Hat		Messner
Paul Bunyan (illustrated by Rockwell Kent)	Esther Shepard	Harcourt, Brace
Dramatized Ballads	Tobitt and White	Dutton
The Saucy Sailor and Other Dramatized Ballads		Dutton
The Dancing Kettle	Yoshiko Uchida	Harcourt, Brace
The Magic Circle	Louis Untermeyer	Knopf

Jim Kjelgaard, author, and Edith Scholl and boys at
Loveland School, Dixon, Illinois

What a world to know!

Publications and News Service, Bowling Green (Ohio) State University

Clara Ingram Judson autographing one of her books for the boys.

Miriam Mason and the children dramatizing her story, "A Pony Called Lightning."

7

Books to Meet Emotional, Esthetic, and Spiritual Needs

*M*UCH of our previous discussion makes it seem as though most children's books are valuable because of their relation to physical and social needs, especially when they are related to subject areas in school curricula. This factor is vital in developing reading children, but perhaps those books which are real literature, regardless of where the story is laid in time or place—those books which develop spiritual awareness, a sense of humor, a growing appreciation of beauty,

179

a sense of integrity, and lasting values—are the most significant books with which today's children can live. The great teacher Elizabeth Nesbitt said in her lecture *Hold to That Which Is Good*, "Literature is immeasurably above and beyond the printed word, of a significance transcending the merely informative, varied as is human destiny, nonexistent without the twin qualities of beauty of idea and beauty of expression."

Many of the books discussed in the last chapter—such as *Little House in the Big Woods, The Good Master, Adam of the Road, And Now Miguel*—are books that will live and live, because of the beauty of their ideas and the beauty of their expression. The fact that children learn much through imitation and identification is readily accepted today. If their family and neighbors set good examples, they are more likely to develop good character qualities. If either their relationship with these people or the people themselves are not good examples, the child's growth into a good citizen is made a more difficult process. Identification and imitation can take place with the fine characters in a book. The human relationships, the quality of the people, and the lasting values in the books considered in this chapter are good.

There are quite a few stories that seven- and eight-year-olds may enjoy reading by themselves. Jerrold Beim has a particular flare for writing stories with appeal for children of this age. Andy, too young to go to school, gets his much-longed-for ride in the school bus in *Andy and the School Bus*. Seth is lucky enough to get a chance to help in his uncle's filling station in *Country Garage*. Frankie proves a brother worth having, even if he is a younger one, in *Kid Brother*. Martha Goldberg really knows how children feel as her readers can perceive in reading *Lunch Box Story, Wait for the Rain*, and *The Twirly Skirt*. So, too, does Sally Scott in her many delightful stories, most of which are about children and their pets. Some of those best loved are *Bobby and His Band, Binky's Fire, Judy's Baby, Sue*

Ann's Busy Day, and *Tippy.* The children have happy as well as exciting adventures in the stories by Lavinia Davis, *Roger and the Fox, Danny's Luck, Summer is Fun,* and *The Wild Birthday Cake.* These four are enhanced by Hildegarde Woodward's illustrations.

Little Quaker Hannah thought her brother had much more chance for fun than she did, but Marguerite De Angeli portrays *both* of them as having quite a good time despite Quaker restrictions in *Thee Hannah.* Her *Copper-Toed Boots* makes real that high moment in any pioneer boy's life when he gets his first copper-toed boots, a sign of approaching manhood. As in all her books, the illustrations make these lovable families real.

Miriam Mason's children are so alive that their problems become the reader's long after he closes the covers of each book, whether it is the Indian boy in *Hominy,* little Jonathan in the book of that name, Caroline in *Caroline and Her Kettle Named Maud,* or the King family in *The Sod House.* Boys will feel genuine kinship with that Kentucky mountain boy who wanted to earn money for his grandmother's Christmas present in Jesse Stuart's *The Beatinest Boy* and *A Penny's Worth of Character,* with Jareb who also lived in the mountains in the book of that name by Miriam Powell, and with Peter from a Vermont farm in Elizabeth Yates' *Mountain Born* and *A Place for Peter.* Girls will feel a similar closeness to Lucinda in Ruth Sawyer's *Roller Skates,* Maggie in her *Maggie Rose,* and the five sisters in a closely-knit New York family of the early 1900's in Sydney Taylor's *All-of-a-Kind Family* and *More All-of-a-Kind Family.* Betsy and Tacy are friends with whom any girl would like to grow up, whether or not she lives in or near Minnesota. She may start with Betsy and Tacy at the age of five in *Betsy-Tacy* by Maud Hart Lovelace and live with Betsy through nine more books to Betsy's marriage in *Betsy's Wedding.* Her growing up experiences which are close to those of many girls are told with naturalness and friendly charm. Some girls may even go to a completely strange environment and still feel kindred in spirit to the little Zulu girl who had real bravery in Reba Mirsky's story of *Thirty-One Brothers and Sisters.*

Older girls understand with their own hearts Brady Allen's discovery when she went to live among strangers in *Home Is Where the Heart Is* as Mildred Pace calls her story. Margueritte Bro and Mary Stolz also are sensitive writers of teen-age novels. Here, again, beauty of idea and expression are combined in *Sarah* by Bro and *Pray Love, Remember,* and others by Mary Stolz.

Nearly every boy and girl in fifth or sixth grade enjoys the Moffatt family whose four children had plenty of fun and excitement at home and at school, summer and winter, in *The Moffatts, Rufus M.* and *The Middle Moffatt* by Eleanor Estes. They sympathize with the problems of a little girl who comes from a poor Polish family with an odd name, but who also is an artist in *One Hundred Dresses* by Eleanor Estes. The Clark family in Vermont have happy times together in *Windy Foot at the County Fair, Sleigh Bells for Windy Foot,* and *Maple Sugar for Windy Foot.* While these stories by Frances Frost are specifically about Toby Clark and his wonderful pony, Windy Foot, they owe much of their enduring charm to their concern with family activities. Sincere respect for personality and sympathetic understanding of problems as well as achievements characterize most of today's fine biographies such as these:

Gandhi, Fighter Without a Sword	Jeanette Eaton
Albert Schweitzer	Joseph Gollomb
Jean Baptiste Pointe de Sable	Shirley Grahame
There Was Once a Slave	
Abraham Lincoln, Friend of the People	Clara Ingram Judson
Nancy Hanks of Wilderness Road	Meridel Le Seuer
Giant of the Yards (Gustavus Swift)	Louise Neyhart
Henry Ford, Engineer	
To a Different Drum: The Story of Henry David Thoreau	Charles Norman
Stormy Victory (Tschaikovsky)	Claire Purdy
The Jacksons of Tennessee	Marguerite Vance

On Wings of Fire: Story of Rose Hawthorne
Lillian Wald   Beryl Williams
Amos Fortune   Elizabeth Yates

In a time of such tension as ours, children are highly sensitive to the fears and insecurities of their parents. They are open targets for all the hair-raising news reporting and propagandizing of radio and television; they are protected very little from the tragedies of hot wars, cold wars, poverty, and suffering. No wonder so many seek relief in something *funny*. The most easily accessible resource is the so-called comic, all too seldom possessing anything comic or humorous. One of their most persistent requests is, "Where are the funny books? I mean books that make you laugh." Many parents are distressed over their children's obsession with comic books, but seldom make much effort to find out what deep-seated need is being met, nor do they have good books of sound basic humor easily available.

The young of all ages laugh at the man's efforts to recover his head in Claire Bishop's *The Man Who Lost His Head*, with funny illustrations by Robert McCloskey; at that wacky duck *Petunia* in Roger Duvoisin's stories and pictures of her crazy adventures; at the silly goose of *Mrs. Goose and Three Ducks* and the other stories by Miriam Clark Potter; at the adventurous monkey in *Curious George* by H. A. Rey; at the gentle bull who loved to smell flowers in *Ferdinand* by Munro Leaf and Robert Lawson; with the little French girl in a convent in *Madeline* by Ludwig Bemelmans; at all the genuine child nonsense in Ruth Krauss' *Hole Is To Dig, How to Make an Earthquake,* and *I'll Be You and You Be Me;* at the inimitable, utterly fantastic pictures and nonsense tales of Dr. Seuss, *Horton Hatches the Egg, Horton Hears a Who, If I Ran the Zoo, And to Think That I Saw It on Mulberry Street,* and *The 500 Hats of Bartholomew Cubbins.*

Ogden Nash has collected some of his favorite humorous verses written by a number of poets in *The Moon Is Shining Bright As Day.* Every child should have the opportunity of laughing over Edward Lear's nonsense verses and limericks in *The Book of Nonsense and More Nonsense*. Many riddles can only be answered by someone with a released sense of humor, so good books of riddles such as *Riddles, Riddles, Riddles* by Joseph Leeming, or *Black Within and Red Without* by Lillian Morrison have perennial appeal.

A few of today's authors have a real sense of humor themselves and know just how to appeal to the sense of humor of a ten- or twelve-year-old. Beverly Cleary's children get themselves into excruciatingly funny situations in *Henry Huggins, Henry and Beezus, Henry and Rickey, Otis Spofford,* and *Ellen Tebbits*. So, also, does Carolyn Haywood's Eddie in *Little Eddie, Eddie's Pay Dirt, Eddie and Gardenia, Eddie and the Fire Engine*. Herbert's hilarious, fabulous adventures are a constant source of enjoyment to his devoted admirers in Hazel Wilson's three books about this boy wonder: *Herbert, Herbert Again, More Fun with Herbert*.

William DuBois mixes a rare group of interests and abilities, some scientific knowledge, great artistic skill, and a marvelous sense of humor to evolve his priceless tales *The Twenty-One Balloons, Peter Graves, The Giant, The Great Geppy,* and *The Flying Locomotive*. Robert Lawson has inside information on some of the characteristics of a few great people which he shares with great fun in his stories of *Ben and Me* (Ben Franklin's mouse's story), *I Discover Columbus* (Columbus's parrot's story), *Mr. Revere and I* (Paul Revere's horse's story). No boy hero is perhaps quite so much fun or quite so much like the average American boy as Robert McCloskey's *Homer Price*. Fun and adventure will be shared with Huck and Tom as long as books are read in those two great classics of American boyhood, *The Adventures of Tom Sawyer* and *The Adventures of Huckleberry Finn* by Mark Twain.

For those children who love real nonsense which also involves animals, Hugh Lofting has created his delightful Dr. Dolittle. There are twelve Dr. Dolittle books. Begin with *The*

Story of Doctor Dolittle, The Voyages of Doctor Dolittle, Doctor Dolittle's Postoffice; few children will stop until they have read all twelve. Walter C. Brooks' amazing farmyard detective, the pig named Freddy, is also popular. Freddy the pig got started back in 1927 by taking Farmer Bean's animals to Florida for the winter, and he has been going strong ever since. There are now twenty Freddy books, including a collection of his poems. It is good to start with the first one, *Freddy Goes to Florida.* His friends are likely to proceed gleefully from the first to the last, *Freddy and the Baseball Team from Mars.* But there may be more in future years. Freddy, once a friend, is always a friend.

Phyllis Fenner has selected choice portions of some of our best humorous writing in her anthology called *Fun, Fun, Fun.* This book has special appeal for older children. Many of her stories provide excellent material for reading aloud to the family or in the classroom.

Most tall tales and many other folk tales are full of humor. Le Grand has a rare facility for spinning a funny yarn out of some tale he has heard here and there in his wanderings through the United States. These tales, which are not long and have vigorous, laugh-producing illustrations by Le Grand himself, have great appeal to slow readers. Here, again, it is important not to categorize them for just such use; they offer sure pleasure to *all* readers. *Cap'n Dow and the Hole in the Doughnut* tells how the hole in the doughnut was invented along the coast of Maine. *Cats for Kansas* tells how Gabe Slade, a trader, managed to get cats for settlers who longed for a cat to purr around the house. *Why Cowboys Sing in Texas* tells the "real" origin of "Yipee yi, Yipee yay!" *When the Mississippi Was Wild* tells how Mike Fink tied the tail of the troublesome alligator in the Mississippi so brave settlers could get across to settle the West. *Tom Benn and Blackbeard, the Pirate* is the amazing story of how Blackbeard, the pirate, was captured, and it comes straight from Ocracoke Inlet in North Carolina. Pecos

Bill, Paul Bunyan, Old Stormalong, Mike Fink and all the rest take any adventurous spirit into adventures tall and taller. The many fine versions of these tales have been discussed in the preceding chapter.

Humor is a saving grace; it is oil on the waters, and it releases tensions. Perhaps, in the last analysis, humor is the long range point of view that sees things in their true relationship. Something that is made too big or too little, exaggerated beyond all reason, made small beyond all possibility or put out of the obvious, accepted pattern evokes laughter. From the laughter comes joy and sight that goes beyond the immediate present to the long view, beyond the far horizon.

Another important characteristic of the good books that build permanent values is that of beauty—as Miss Nesbitt said, "beauty of idea, beauty of expression." Here are three quotations from poetry written by children in Florida elementary schools:

> "But when the light begins to fade
> And my steps are homeward made
> It is with a glad but peaceful mind
> That I can such beauty find."

> "No tree is quite so beautiful
> As the weeping willow tree,
> And though it seems to be so sad
> It makes my heart feel free."

> "When the gray clouds
> Open their gray eyes
> They start to cry.
> The bright orange sun comes out.
> The clouds stop crying.
> The sun laughs at them.
> He never cries,
> The beautiful sun never cries."

To the first child, finding beauty is associated with "a glad and peaceful mind"; to the second child, beauty brings a sense of freedom; to the third child beauty means joy and laughter. You and I could add many more values that would enter a child's horizon if he had the opportunity to develop his appreciation of beauty. It is good to think of little children being sensitively aware of these three great values in life: peace, freedom, and joy. But one notices that in each of these three instances, the beauty is found in the outdoor world. There is plenty of beauty in our land still for children to observe: shining blue waters lapping the shell-strewn sandy shores at Florida; Georgia's tall pines and gently swaying, gray, green moss; New England's green-clad hills and rock-bound shores; Pennsylvania's laurel-covered mountains; Wisconsin's beautiful small lakes; the tapestry of color in the north woods on a shining October day; Arizona's carpet of exquisite spring flowers in the desert; California's majestic Sierras and colorful fruit valleys; Oregon's apple orchards, lily fields, and mountains sloping down to the sea. America's physical beauty is there to behold for all who have eyes to see.

But what of all that our children look at when they are inside—home, school, shop, or building? What sort of taste does the average Main Street in America offer? Many homes? Too many schools? What do our children look at in the average school room that, by hook or crook, can be thought of as satisfying their need for beauty—beauty in color, beauty in line, beauty in pattern and design, beauty in word, "beauty for to touch, for to see."

Joel walked around a book exhibit slowly, opening and shutting one book after another, mostly those in the social studies section, not the more colorful picture book section. His eyes were wide with wonder and his voice had a note of awe as he said, "I never knew geography could be so beautiful." The twins, who are seven, go to a two-room school in a small village. They belong to that tidal wave of children who overflow every first grade to twice and three times its capacity. A basement room was fixed up for them. Walls and floors all over the school are battleship gray—now well scuffed. Old fly-specked maps and three ugly steel engravings are on the wall. A few shelves have old, worn textbooks—backs ragged and torn—piled on them. There is a piano in one room with ivory keys so dirty that it is hard to believe they are not ebony like the black keys. In the tiny corridor, however, stands a bright red and brighter chromium *coke machine*—the only clean or colorful or shining thing in that whole school!

The twins, like all other children in that school and like some of the parents and teachers and most older brothers and sisters read comics one or two hours every day. They pore over the ugly, distorted drawings and hideous colors printed on cheap, mottled, newsprint paper. Where are the resources to build peace, freedom, and joy on the inside, within the pattern of life that surrounds so many of our American children with such ugliness? Of course, there are exceptions. There are some beautiful schools with clean rest-rooms, auditoriums, libraries, good pictures, and audio-visual equipment. There are beautiful homes, even beautiful shops, mostly in cities and resorts.

In art, most schools no longer use hectograph designs to be filled in or give out patterns of fall leaves and spring tulips to be traced and cut out. Instead, children are given large pieces of paper and plenty of chalk, crayons, and poster paint in beautiful colors and encouraged to draw not only what they see, but what they feel. And wherever free expression is encouraged, the results astonish us—such beauty! In music, there is more free rhythmic play, more listening to good music, more singing, more chances to play with instruments. Many children know and love not only the tunes on the hit parade, but also some Mozart, Haydn, MacDowell, and Stravinsky. In language arts, the written and spoken word, there is encouragement of more observation of things to tell and write about, more opportunity to see all kinds of books for fun and fantasy, joy and imagination, information and inspiration. There are books telling stories in English so beautiful that the words engrave a pattern in the mind; books of poetry, with words that sing themselves into your very being; books with pictures drawn by artists, real artists sharing beauty in their various media of lithograph, water color, engraving, crayon, pen and ink, and pencil and opening doors to beauty. Some of these books have true distinction. The binding, the color of the paper, the kind of type, the reproduction of the artist's pictures, the design of the title page, end papers, and jacket all harmonize with the content in such a way that this combination of content and format gives one a true experience of beauty and arouses a *whole* response.

Some of the picture storybooks of our generation give children the opportunity to live with beauty to the extent that it becomes a very part of their being, on the inside, on the outside. There is neither time nor space to discuss in detail what it means to look at and feel the beauty of Leonard Weisgard's pictures of the cycle of seasons in *The Little Island,* the story of which is a wonderful first step in helping a child to know what faith is. *For little children?* Actually it is ageless, as are all things which are of the spirit. This is true also of *Leif the Lucky* by the d'Aulaires. A whole sense of man's desire to go forth to explore his world is in that picture of the boy Leif holding the prow of his father's ship. How could one sense more poignantly family love than in Politi's charming story of *Juanita,* whose parents named their shop for her because they loved her so much? One likes to consider the inner core of beauty in all these books. The children who live with them find it themselves.

	Author	Illustrator
Tim to the Rescue	Ardizzone	Ardizzone
Madeleine	Bemelmans	Bemelmans
Cinderella	Marcia Brown	Brown
Two Little Trains	Margaret Wise Brown	Charlot
A Child's Good Morning		
Child's Good Night Book		
Young Kangaroo		Shimin

The Little House	Burton	Burton
In My Mother's House	Clark	Herrera
Ola	d'Aulaire	d'Aulaire
Leif the Lucky		
Abraham Lincoln		
Pocahontas		
Christopher Columbus		
Story of Babar	de Brunhoff	de Brunoff
Thank You Book	Francoise	Francoise
Noel for Jeanne Marie		
Millions of Cats	Gag	Gag
Look:	Gay	Gay
Wonderful Things		
Mei Li	Handforth	Handforth
Who Goes There?	Lathrop	Lathrop
Little Island	MacDonald	Weisgard
Little Lost Lamb		
Make Way for Ducklings	McCloskey	McCloskey
One Morning in Maine		
Juanita	Politi	Politi
Pedro, Angel of Olvera Street		
Rain Drop Splash	Tresselt	Weisgard
White Snow, Bright Snow		Duvoisin
Follow the Wind		
Wake Up Farm		
Pumpkin Moonshine	Tudor	Tudor
Snow for Christmas		
Whose Birthday Is It?	N. Watson	A. Watson

It is interesting to note how often the author is also the artist. The creative spirit often finds expression in more than one medium. Most of these authors have many more books than the few mentioned here, all well worth the knowing. Many other beautiful books have been mentioned under other headings. As children grow older, illustrations are not always included. Often a frontispiece or chapter heading lend beauty. Selection of type and paper and the overall designing of a book have significance. The children who live with some of the following books will be truly walking with beauty, even as the Indian chant says:

With beauty before me I walk,
With beauty behind me I walk,
With beauty all around me I walk,
With beauty I walk.

	Author	Illustrator
Hill of Little Miracles	Angelo	Angelo
The Forest Pool	Armer	Armer
Big Tree	Buff	Buff
Dancing Cloud		
Dash and Dart		
Beyond the Paw Paw Trees	Brown	Brown
Secret of the Andes	Clark	Charlot
Santiago		
The Blue Cat	Coblentz	Holland
Abraham Lincoln	Daugherty	Daugherty
Daniel Boone		
Wheel on the School	De Jong	Sendak
The Silver Curlew	Farjeon	Shephard
Legend of Paul Bunyan	Felton	Bennett
Augustus Caesar's World	Foster	Foster
Blue Willow	Gates	Lantz
Deep Flowing Brook	Goss	Blaisdell
Wind in the Willows	Grahame	Shepard
Adam of the Road	Gray	Morse
Paddle-to-the-Sea	Holling	Holling
Tales of the Pampas	Hudson	Duvoisin
Victorian Cinderella (Harriet Beecher Stowe)	Jackson	Means
Hidden Treasure of Glaston	Jewett	Chapman
And Now Miguel	Krumgold	Charlot
Little Brother of the Wilderness	Le Seuer	Alden
The Mother Ditch	La Farge	Larsson
Song of Robin Hood	Malcolmson	Burton
Gandhi's Story	Masani	Masani
Homer Price	McCloskey	McCloskey
Ol' Paul	Rounds	Rounds
The Story of Peer Gynt	Sandys	Eichenberg
The Long Christmas	Sawyer	Angelo
Roller Skates		
The White Stag	Seredy	Seredy
The Good Master		

North Star Shining (History of American Negroes)	Swift	Ward
Li Lun, Lad of Courage	Treffinger	Kurt Wiese
Elizabeth Tudor: Sovereign Lady	Vance	Walker
Little House in the Big Woods	Wilder	Williams

Classics

Children's classics are a group of books, some of which originally were written for children, others for anyone who reads. Children take them to their hearts because of their universal appeal in terms of life, humor, beauty, and integrity. There should never be a fixed list of these books, for *Millions of Cats* will surely be added to *The Tale of Peter Rabbit* as a classic for younger children, and *Little House in the Big Woods* takes its place with *Heidi* and *Hans Brinker*. It just takes time to acquire the label "classic." Since most of these classics are in the public domain, they are published in a variety of editions, many of which are well edited, well designed, and often beautifully illustrated. Classics possess the qualities which make a book live, but it is a serious mistake to think that every child must read all the classics in order to be properly educated or literate or well read. The classics are as wide as life, with a variety of appeal. Some are for certain readers, some for others. It is rare that a child will read all the classics. Many children, even many adults, never really know what *Alice in Wonderland* is all about. But some do, and for these there is all the wonder, nonsense, insight, and pure delight of Alice. Certain books such as *Wind in the Willows* are not easy for many children to enjoy by themselves, but when read aloud by an understanding adult, they become books to be read and reread, savored and enjoyed. There are some families who read together ". . . the piper at the gates of dawn . . ." every year on one of the first mornings when one sees signs of spring. *Winnie-the-Pooh* is likewise not for every child, but some families read Eeyore's birthday as a part of the birthday celebration of every member of the family. This is wonderful for that kind of family, but not all families celebrate this way, nor should they; there are "ways and ways." It therefore is exceedingly important not to put certain books on a required list for everyone. One sure way to kill interest in many a good book is to put it on a "must" list. Not everyone, even highly literate people, agree on what belongs in such a list, but the following books are included in most bibliographies of so-called children's classics.

For very young children, Beatrix Potter's *Tale of Peter Rabbit* and her many other delightful tales and pictures of small animals are surely classics, as is Helen Bannerman's *Little Black Sambo,* despite some quite irrelevant discussion of this pure nonsense tale involving racial prejudices. Miss Mulock's *Little Lame Prince* and *Adventures of a Brownie* are still much loved. Fables, fairy tales, legends, and myths should be part of everyone's heritage.

Fables	Aesop
Fables	La Fontaine
Fairy Tales	Andersen
Household Tales	Grimm
Iliad	Homer
The Odyssey	

The Norse and Greek myths have been discussed previously. There are other stories which live on and on and surely deserve to be called classics. We should hope that many children will read them, but let us not be anxiously determined that all must do so. These titles are more often read by children between the ages of ten and thirteen.

East of the Sun and West of the Moon	Asbjornsen
Alice in Wonderland	Carroll
Through the Looking Glass	
Pinocchio	Collodi
Robinson Crusoe	Defoe
Hans Brinker	Dodge
Smoky	James

Jungle Books	Kipling
At the Back of the North Wind	MacDonald
Black Beauty	Sewell
Heidi	Spyri
Treasure Island	Stevenson
Tom Sawyer	Twain
Adventures of Huckleberry Finn	
Twenty Thousand Leagues under the Sea	Verne

Robin Hood and King Arthur are retold by several distinguished writers. Howard Pyle's Robin Hood and four volumes of King Arthur legends are especially beautiful. There is an excellent Robin Hood by Gilbert, and both the Lanier and McLeod versions of King Arthur are good.

The following classics are more often of interest to older children.

Little Women	Alcott
Little Men	
Arabian Nights	Ansley
Song of Roland	Baldwin
Lorna Doone	Blackmore
Last of the Mohicans	Cooper
A Tale of Two Cities	Dickens
Three Musketeers	Dumas
Legend of Sleepy Hollow	Irving
Alhambra	
The Heroes	Kingsley
Westward Ho!	
Tales from Shakespeare	Lamb
Gold Bug and Other Tales	Poe
Ivanhoe	Scott
Quentin Durward	
Gulliver's Travels	Swift
Swiss Family Robinson	Wyss

There are an increasing number of books about art and artists which help develop a child's art appreciation. Two biographies of the artists Giotto and Millet are beautifully done by Opal Wheeler and Sybil Deucher: *Giotto Tended the Sheep* and

Millet Tended the Soil. The Animal's Frolic is a tribute to the vision of a group of people; it is the reproduction of the original twelfth century scroll by Toba Sojo of Japan with monkeys, rabbits, and frogs romping merrily through a feast day. Velma Varner has added fitting, simple narration. Hans Bauman tells the great adventure of the four boys who discovered the ice age cave in France in *The Caves of the Great Hunters*. There are excellent drawings of these examples of prehistoric art. Here is excitement, adventure, history, archaeology, art, and beauty all rolled into one book; it will satisfy a variety of needs and interests of many a child.

Made in Mexico by Patricia Fent Ross and *Made in China* by Cornelia Spencer are two distinctive books in a group of "Made in" books, each one about the arts and crafts of a country. Each is written by a person who has lived long in the country and knows the people—their life, their crafts, their arts. Actually, each is a cultural history of the country, including excellent reproductions of much of their best art expression. Here is enriching reading for the child sensitive enough to realize that understanding people through knowledge of their needs, desires, and aspirations in a variety of art forms can be a key to perspective. Since this book is primarily concerned with reading, we will call attention to only such art books as are primarily concerned with art forms or great pictures or sculpture, without including the many fine "how to do it" books.

House of a Hundred Windows	Brown
Famous Paintings	Chase
Discovery of Design	Donner
Pictures to Grow Up With	Gibson
More Pictures to Grow Up With	
Michelangelo	Ripley
Leonardo da Vinci	
Vincent Van Gogh	
Rembrandt	

Ripley's books are beautiful biographical studies of these artists, with excellent reproductions of their work.

In the realm of music, many children enjoy music inspired by a story, such as *The Sorcerer's Apprentice* by Dukas or *Peter and the Wolf* by Prokofieff, if they know the tale which the music narrates. Prokofieff, himself, has told *Peter and the Wolf*, with added explanations of which instrument represents which character and the themes that are characteristic of each. David Cooke and Richard Rostron each tell the enchanting tale of *The Sorcerer's Apprentice* in beautiful books. Children enjoy hearing an orchestra play much more if they know the instruments—strings, woodwinds, brass, and percussion. There are several books about orchestras, each quite different in approach, from the clear photographs and simple text of Harriet Huntington's *Tune Up* to the delightful humor and sophistication of Balet's *What Makes an Orchestra*.

What Makes an Orchestra	Balet
Making an Orchestra	Commins
Tune Up	Huntington
Picture Book of Musical Instruments	Lacey
From These Comes Music	Stoddard

Many children hear and perform music better if they know something of the lives and backgrounds of composers. Many of the biographies of great musicians have been discussed with other biographies in the previous chapter.

> The poet's a sensitive man
> Close to the rhythmic core of his world,
> So he tells what he feels,
> Tells the inside not the outside of experience.

Most children are close to the rhythmic core of the world. Their speech is often poetic in form. Most of them know almost intuitively what the poet is saying, for we live in a rhythmic universe which is hot and cold, dry and moist, dark and light. Rocking is a natural way to soothe a child, for it places him in the world's rhythmic pattern. So, too, does the poetry he first hears, whether it be Mother Goose rhymes or the amusing couplets of *Johnny Crow's Garden* by Leslie Brooks. There are many beautiful editions of Mother Goose, several of which are listed at the end of the chapter, from Rojankovsky's *Tall Mother Goose* to Marguerite De Angeli's exquisite *Book of Nusery and Mother Goose Rhymes*. Christina Rossetti is especially dear to the child who loves the outdoor world in her *Sing Song* poems.[1]

> "Who has seen the wind?
> Neither I nor you:
> But when the leaves hang trembling
> The wind is passing thro'."

Harry Behn also knows a child's special loves, as anyone will discover by reading aloud to children of all ages *The Little Hill, Windy Morning,* or *All Kinds of Time.* James Tippett seems to catch a child's response to everyday experiences over and over in *I Go-A-Traveling, I Live in the City, I Know Some Little Animals.* Stevenson's *Child's Garden of Verses* belongs to every child. Many a child is glad that Christopher Robin was the son of A. A. Milne, who caught the rhythm and delight of a small child's feelings in the poems for and about Christopher in *When We Were Very Young* and *Now We are Six.* Another of the special poets for children, Eleanor Farjeon comes from England. All of her poems—for everyday and Christmas—are now gathered into one volume, *Eleanor Farjeon's Poems for Children.* Rose Fyleman's *Fairies and Chimneys* is for the child who delights in the little people. William Blake's *Songs of Innocence* and Walter de La Mare's *Collected Poems* and *A Child's Day* are for the "spirit's pure delight."

Read poetry aloud to children, with children; it is of their very being. It sings its way into their innermost hearts and minds, even as it becomes the extension of their hearts and minds.

"I know."

"I feel it too."

"That's me."

[1] Christina Rossetti, from *Sing Song* (New York: Macmillan, 1952).

"Read it again."

"Let me say it too."

These are characteristic responses from the listening child.

The child who hears poetry from the time he first listens to anything loves it, probably first for its rhythm, later for its feeling or its sensitive catching of words. For the child who has always heard poetry, it can never become something hard to understand or "sissy," or peculiarly literary or abstruse. Let us not dissect and bisect and vivisect it too much in searching for meaning. The true poet speaks in his own way to each individual. We must not force memorization, especially group memorization, for it can so easily destroy the individual response to the thousand shades of meaning and mood. Let the poetry which comes from life flow through the listener and the reader, and then return into life itself.

As the child grows, he comes to know Longfellow, Whittier, Bryant, Emerson, Benét, Whitman, Robert Frost, Edwin Arlington Robinson, Robert P. Tristram Coffin, Robinson Jeffers, and Carl Sandburg, as well as Emliy Dickinson and Edna St. Vincent Millay—Americans all. The English poets, too, have meaning for him: Keats, Shelly, Wordsworth, Tennyson, Kipling, and Noyes. Many of the best loved poems of all these poets are gathered into good anthologies such as these:

For Young Children

Sung under the Silver Umbrella	Association for Childhood Education
A Small Child's Book of Verse	Pelagie Doane
Very Young Verses	Geismer and Suder
For a Child	Wilma McFarland

For Children of All Ages

The Winged Horse Anthology	Joseph Auslander
Gaily We Parade	John and Sarah Brewton
Under the Tent of the Sky	Brewton

Bridled with Rainbows	
Sing a Song of Seasons	
My Poetry Book	Huffard and Carlisle
A Pocketful of Rhymes	Katherine Love
100 Story Poems	Elinor Parker
100 Poems about People	
Silver Pennies	Blanche Thompson
The Magic Circle	Louis Untermeyer
Rainbow in the Sky	
Stars to Steer By	
This Singing World	

In the broadest sense of the word, all of these books of beauty, humor, integrity—whether in prose or poetry—contribute to a child's spiritual growth. The great religions of the world represent man's highest spiritual aspirations and his need for a supreme being. In the occidental world, these religions are chiefly Jewish and Christian; in the orient, there are Mohammedanism, Buddhism, Hinduism, Taoism, and others. A beautiful, simple book about God as a supreme being, not as a specific god worshipped according to a certain religion, is Florence Fitch's *Book about God,* beautifully illustrated by Leonard Weisgard. The Petershams have caught the very essence of the Palestinian family and countryside in their illustrations for *The Christ Child,* which uses the Luke story of the birth of Jesus. There are a number of children's Bibles, some one of which may meet the various needs of different children.

The Living Bible: A Shortened Version for Modern Readers	Ballou
The Lord Is My Shepherd	Barnes
A Small Child's Bible (Protestant and Catholic)	Doane
The Junior Bible	Goodspeed
Children's Bible	Sherman and Kent
The Book of Books	Sypherd

Elizabeth Orton Jones has pictures truly child-like, interpreting selected verses from the Old and New Testaments in

Small Rain. In *This Is the Way,* she catches the same, character-istic, child feeling with sensitivity in her pictures interpreting passages from many great religions of the world, selected by Jessie Orton Jones. Florence Fitch describes the ways of wor-ship of the Jewish, Catholic, and Protestant faiths in *One God.* The beautiful photographs in this invaluable book help children grow in sympathy with ways of worship other than their own. She has widened horizons to the orient in *Their Search for God—Ways of Worship in the Orient* and *Allah: The God of Islam—Moslem Life and Worship.* Delight Ansley also tells the stories of different approaches to God in *The Good Ways.* Ruth Smith has collected sacred writings from many peoples in a beautiful and distinguished book, *The Tree of Life.* Needless to say, these books about comparative religion are not of interest to all children; but for those who are ready for them, it is good to know that such books can meet them at their present stage of spiritual development and contribute to their future growth.

For Christian people, Christmas is the high peak of the year. There are many excellent collections of Christmas stories, as well as individual stories about the first Christmas or Christmas today and interesting books describing customs and ways of celebration in our own and other lands. Pictures of deep sensi-tivity as well as sincere, simple text characterize several Christ-mas stories for young children.

	Author	*Illustrator*
Christmas in the Barn	Margaret Brown	Barbara Cooney
The Little Fir Tree		
The First Christmas	Robbie Trent	Marc Simont
Whose Birthday Is It?	Nancy Watson	Aldronsa Watson
The Animals Came First	Jean Welch	Ruth Carroll

Alta Halverson Seymour has several Christmas stories, each characteristic of Christmas in a different country:

Kaatji and the Christmas Compass (Holland)
The Christmas Donkey (France)
Arne and the Christmas Star (Norway)
The Christmas Stove (Switzerland)

Nora Unwin's lively drawings literally illumine Elizabeth Yates' sensitive story of a little Vermont farm boy, David, who finds out whether the old legend that animals speak human language at midnight on Christmas eve is really true in *Once in the Year*. Alice Dalgliesh has collected many choice stories and poems in her book entitled *Christmas*. Ruth Sawyer tells of many Christmas customs in *This Way to Christmas,* and of Maggie's special Christmas birthday in *Maggie Rose*. Valenti Angelo's distinctive line drawings enhance her collection of twelve Christmas tales—one for each of the twelve days of Christmas—and some unusual carols called *The Long Christmas*. One of the most loved of all carols is "The Twelve Days of Christmas." Ilonka Karasz has an illustration for each of the twelve days in delicate pastel colors in a beautiful book, *The Twelve Days of Christmas*.

Many families read Dickens' *Christmas Carol* together each year.

Every child with a Christian heritage should hear the Christmas story, preferably as told in the Gospel according to St. Luke. It is good for families to read together. Some children enjoy becoming the reader for the family as they grow in their enjoyment of reading. Reading is for all the year—every day and holidays—because literature is "varied as is human destiny" and can help a child both find his destiny as well as ways to fulfill it.

Books Discussed in Chapter 7

Fables	Aesop	Garden City
Fables		Grosset & Dunlap
Little Women	Louisa M. Alcott	Little, Brown

Fairy Tales	Hans Christian Andersen	Grosset & Dunlap
Little Men	Valenti Angelo	Crowell
The Hill of Little Miracles		Viking
The Good Ways	Delight Ansley	Crowell
Arabian Nights		Grosset & Dunlap
Tim to the Rescue	Edward Ardizzone	Oxford
The Forest Pool	Laura Adams Armer	Longmans, Green
East of the Sun and West of the Moon	P. S. Asbjornsen	Macmillan
Sung under the Silver Umbrella	Association for Childhood Education	Macmillan
Winged Horse Anthology	Joseph Auslander	Doubleday
Miss Hickory	Caroline S. Bailey	Viking
Song of Roland	James Baldwin	Scribner
What Makes an Orchestra	Jan Balet	Oxford
The Living Bible	Robert O. Ballou	Viking
Little Black Sambo	Helen Bannerman	Lippincott
The Lord Is My Shepherd	Nancy Barnes	Scribner
Caves of the Great Hunters	Hans Bauman	Pantheon
The Little Hill	Harry Behn	Harcourt, Brace
Windy Morning		Harcourt, Brace
All Kinds of Time		Harcourt, Brace
Andy and the School Bus	Jerrold Beim	Harcourt, Brace
Country Garage		Morrow
Kid Brother		Morrow
Madeleine	Ludwig Bemelmans	Viking
The Man Who Lost His Head	Claire H. Bishop	Viking
Lorna Doone	R. D. Blackmore	Dutton
Songs of Innocence	William Blake	Holt
Gaily We Parade	John and Sara Brewton	Macmillan
Under the Tent of the Sky		Macmillan
Bridled with Rainbows		Macmillan
Sing a Song of Seasons		Macmillan
Sarah	Margueritte Bro	Doubleday
Johnny Crow's Garden	Leslie Brooks	Warne

Freddy Goes to Florida (and others)	Walter Brooks	Knopf
Cinderella	Marcia Brown	Scribner
Two Little Trains	Margaret Wise Brown	Scott
Child's Good Morning Book		Scott
Child's Good Night		Scott
House of a Hundred Windows		Harper
Christmas in the Barn		Crowell
The Little Fir Tree		Crowell
Young Kangaroo		Scott
Beyond the Paw Paw Trees	Palmer Brown	Harper
Dancing Cloud	Conrad and Mary Buff	Viking
Dash and Dart		Viking
Big Tree		Viking
The Little House	Virginia Lee Burton	Houghton Mifflin
Alice in Wonderland	Lewis Carroll	Grosset & Dunlap
Through the Looking Glass		
Famous Paintings	Alice Chase	Platt and Munk
In My Mother's House	Ann Nolan Clark	Viking
Secret of the Andes		Viking
Santiago		Viking
Henry Huggins	Beverly Cleary	Morrow
Henry and Beezus		Morrow
Henry and Ribsy		Morrow
Otis Spofford		Morrow
Ellen Tibbitts		Morrow
The Blue Cat	C. C. Coblentz	Longmans, Green
Pinocchio	Carlo Collodi	Grosset & Dunlap
Making an Orchestra	D. B. Commins	Macmillan
The Sorcerer's Apprentice	David Cooke	Winston
The Last of the Mohicans	James Fenimore Cooper	Scribner
Christmas	Alice Dalgliesh	Scribner
Abraham Lincoln	James Daugherty	Viking

Daniel Boone		Viking
Leif the Lucky	Edgar and Ingri d'Aulaire	Doubleday
Ola		Doubleday
Abraham Lincoln		Doubleday
Pocahontas		Doubleday
Christopher Columbus		Doubleday
Danny's Luck	Lavinia Davis	Doubleday
Roger and the Fox		Doubleday
Summer Is Fun		Doubleday
Wild Birthday Cake		Doubleday
Copper Toed Boots	Marguerite De Angeli	Doubleday
Thee Hannah		Doubleday
Story of Babar	Jean de Brunhoff	Random House
Robinson Crusoe	Daniel Defoe	Grosset & Dunlap
Wheel on the School	Meindert De Jong	Harper
Collected Poems	Walter de La Mare	Holt
A Child's Day		Holt
Christmas Carol	Charles Dickens	Grosset & Dunlap
A Tale of Two Cities		Scribner
A Small Child's Bible	Pelagie Doane	Oxford
A Small Child's Book of Verse		Oxford
Hans Brinker	Mary Mapes Dodge	Grosset & Dunlap
Discovering Design	Marion Downer	Lothrop, Lee & Shepard
Twenty-one Balloons	William Pene Dubois	Viking
Peter Graves		Viking
The Giant		Viking
The Great Geppy		Viking
The Flying Locomotive		Viking
The Three Musketeers	Alexandre Dumas	Grosset & Dunlap
Petunia	Roger Duvoisin	Knopf
Gandhi, Fighter without a Sword	Jeanette Eaton	Morrow

The Moffats	Eleanor Estes	Harcourt, Brace
The Middle Moffat		Harcourt, Brace
Rufus M.		Harcourt, Brace
One Hundred Dresses		Harcourt, Brace
Eleanor Farjeon's Poems for Children	Eleanor Farjeon	Lippincott
The Silver Curlew		Viking
Legend of Paul Bunyan	Harold Felton	Knopf
Fun, Fun, Fun (and others)	Phyllis Fenner	Watts
Book about God	Florence M. Fitch	Lothrop, Lee & Shepard
One God: The Ways We Worship Him		Lothrop, Lee & Shepard
Their Search for God		Lothrop, Lee & Shepard
The God of Islam		Lothrop, Lee & Shepard
Augustus Caesar's World	Genevieve Foster	Scribner
Thank You Book	Francoise	Scribner
Noel for Jeanne Marie		Scribner
Windy Foot at the County Fair	Frances Frost	Whittlesey House
Sleighbells for Windy Foot		Whittlesey House
Maple Sugar for Windy Foot		Whittlesey House
Fairies and Chimneys	Rose Fyleman	Doubleday
Millions of Cats	Wanda Gag	Coward
Gone Is Gone		Coward
Blue Willow	Doris Gates	Viking
Look!	Zhenya Gay	Viking
Wonderful Things		Viking
Very Young Verses	Barbara P. Geismer and Antoinette Suter	Houghton Mifflin
Pictures to Grow Up With	Katherine Gibson	Studio
More Pictures to Grow Up With		Studio
Robin Hood	Henry Gilbert	Lippincott
The Lunch Box Story	Martha Goldberg	Holiday House
Wait for the Rain		Holiday House

Twirly Skirt		Holiday House
Albert Schweitzer	Joseph Gollomb	Vanguard
The Junior Bible	Edgar Goodspeed	Macmillan
Deep Flowing Brook: Story of Johann Sebastian Bach	Madeleine Goss	Holt
Jean Baptiste Pointe de Sable	Shirley Graham	Messner
There Was Once a Slave		Messner
Wind in the Willows	Kenneth Grahame	Scribner
Adam of the Road	Elizabeth J. Gray	Viking
Household Tales	Grimm Brothers	Macmillan
Tales from Grimm (illustrated by Gag)		Coward
Grimm's Fairy Tales		Grosset & Dunlap
Mei Li	Thomas Handforth	Doubleday
Little Eddie	Caroline Haywood	Morrow
Eddie's Pay Dirt		Morrow
Eddie and Gardenia		Morrow
Eddie and the Fire Engine		Morrow
Paddle-to-the-Sea	Holling C. Holling	Houghton Mifflin
Iliad	Homer	Macmillan
Odyssey		Macmillan
Tales of the Pampas	W. H. Hudson	Knopf
My Poetry Book	Huffard and Carlisle	Winston
Tune Up	Harriet Huntington	Doubleday
The Legend of Sleepy Hollow	Washington Irving	Houghton Mifflin
Alhambra		Houghton Mifflin
Victorian Cinderella	Phyllis Wynn Jackson	Holiday House
Smoky	Will James	Scribner
Hidden Treasure of Glaston	Eleanore Jewett	Viking
Small Rain	Jessie Orton Jones	Viking
This Is the Way		Viking
Abraham Lincoln, Friend of the People	Clara Ingram Judson	Follett

The Twelve Days of Christmas	Ilonka Karasz	Harper
The Heroes	Charles Kingsley	Macmillan
Jungle Books	Rudyard Kipling	Doubleday
A Hole Is to Dig	Ruth Krauss	Harper
How to Make an Earthquake		Harper
I'll Be You and You Be Me		Harper
And Now Miguel	Joseph Krumgold	Crowell
Picture Book of Musical Instruments	Marion Lacey	Lothrop, Lee & Shepard
The Mother Ditch	Oliver La Farge	Houghton Mifflin
Fables (translated by M. W. Brown)	Jean de La Fontaine	Harper
Tales from Shakespeare	Charles and Mary Lamb	Macmillan
The Boys' King Arthur	Sidney Lanier	Scribner
Who Goes There?	Dorothy Lathrop	Macmillan
Ben and Me	Robert Lawson	Little, Brown
I Discover Columbus		Little, Brown
Mr. Revere and I		Little, Brown
Ferdinand	Munro Leaf	Viking
Book of Nonsense and More Nonsense	Edward Lear	Dodd, Mead
Riddles, Riddles, Riddles	Joseph F. Leeming	Watts
Cap'n Dow and the Hole in the Doughnut	Le Grand	Abingdon
Cats for Kansas		Abingdon
Why Cowboys Sing in Texas		Abingdon
When the Mississippi Was Wild		Abingdon
Tom Benn and Blackbeard the Pirate		Abingdon
Little Brother of the Wilderness	Meridel Le Sueur	Knopf
The Story of Dr. Doolittle	Hugh Lofting	Lippincott
Voyages of Dr. Doolittle		Lippincott
Dr. Doolittle's Post Office		Lippincott
Pocketful of Rhymes	Katherine Love	Crowell

Betsy Tacy	Maud Hart Lovelace	Crowell
Betsy's Wedding		Crowell
At the Back of the North Wind	George MacDonald	Macmillan
Little Island	Golden MacDonald	Doubleday
Little Lost Lamb		Doubleday
Homer Price	Robert McCloskey	Viking
Make Way for Ducklings		Viking
One Morning in Maine		Viking
For a Child	Wilma McFarland	Westminster
Book of King Arthur and His Noble Knights	Mary McLeod	Lippincott
Song of Robin Hood	Anne Malcolmson	Houghton Mifflin
Gandhi's Story	Shakuntala Masani	Oxford
Susannah the Pioneer Cow	Miriam Mason	Macmillan
Caroline and Her Kettle Named Maud		Macmillan
Hominy		Macmillan
Little Jonathan		Macmillan
Sugarbush Family		Macmillan
Winnie the Pooh	A. A. Milne	Dutton
House at Pooh Corner		Dutton
When We Were Very Young		Dutton
Now We Are Six		Dutton
Thirty-one Brothers and Sisters	Reba Mirsky	Follett
Seven Grandmothers		Follett
Black Within and Red Without	Lillian Morrison	Crowell
Mother Goose (illustrated by M. De Angeli)		Doubleday
Tall Mother Goose (illustrated by Rojankovsky)		Harper
Picture Book of Mother Goose (illustrated by Petersham)		Coward

Adventures of a Brownie	Dinah Craik Mulock	Macmillan
The Little Lame Prince		Macmillan
The Moon Is Shining Bright as Day	Ogden Nash	Lippincott
Henry Ford, Engineer	Louise Neyhart	Houghton Mifflin
Giant of the Yards (Gustavus Swift)		Houghton Mifflin
To a Different Drum (Thoreau)	Charles Norman	Harper
Home Is Where the Heart Is	Mildred Mastin Pace	Whittlesey House
100 Story Poems	Elinor Parker	Crowell
100 Poems about People		Crowell
The Christ Child	Maud and Miska Petersham	Doubleday
The Gold Bug	Edgar Allen Poe	Macmillan
Juanita	Leo Politi	Scribner
Pedro the Angel of Olvera Street		Scribner
The Tale of Peter Rabbit	Beatrix Potter	Warne
The Tale of Jemima Puddleduck		Warne
The Tale of Squirrel Nutkin		Warne
Mrs. Goose and Three Ducks	Miriam Clark Potter	Lippincott
Jareb	Miriam Powell	Crowell
Peter and the Wolf	Sergei Prokofieff	Knopf
Stormy Victory (Tchaikowsky)	Claire Purdy	Messner
Some Merry Adventures of Robin Hood	Howard Pyle	Scribner
The Story of King Arthur and His Knights		Scribner
Curious George	H. A. Rey	Houghton Mifflin
Leonardo da Vinci	Elizabeth Ripley	Oxford
Michelangelo		Oxford
Rembrandt		Oxford
Vincent Van Gogh		Oxford

Made in Mexico	Patricia Fent Ross	Knopf
Sing Song	Christina Rossetti	Macmillan
The Sorcerer's Apprentice	Richard Rostron	Morrow
Ol' Paul	Glen Rounds	Holiday
The Story of Peer Gynt	E. V. Sandys	Crowell
Maggie Rose	Ruth Sawyer	Harper
Roller Skates		Viking
The Long Christmas		Viking
This Way to Christmas		Harper
Bobby and His Band	Sally Scott	Harcourt, Brace
Binky's Fire		Harcourt, Brace
Judy's Baby		Harcourt, Brace
Sue Ann's Busy Day		Harcourt, Brace
Tippy		Harcourt, Brace
Ivanhoe	Sir Walter Scott	Dodd, Mead
Quentin Durward		Scribner
The Good Master	Kate Seredy	Viking
The White Stag		Viking
Horton Hatches the Egg	Dr. Seuss	Random House
Horton Hears a Who		Random House
If I Ran the Zoo		Random House
On Beyond Zebra		Random House
And to Think That I Saw It on Mulberry Street		
The 500 Hats of Bartholomew Cubbins		Vanguard Vanguard
Black Beauty	Helen Sewell	Grosset & Dunlap
Kattji and the Christmas Compass	Alta Seymour	Follett
The Christmas Donkey		Follett
Arne and the Christmas Star		Follett
The Christmas Stove		Follett
Children's Bible (illustrated by Taylor)	Sherman and Kent	Scribner
The Tree of Life	Ruth Smith	Viking
The Animal's Frolic	Toja Sojo	Putnam
Made in China	Cornelia Spencer	Knopf

Heidi	Johanna Spyri	Grosset & Dunlap
A Child's Garden of Verses	Robert Louis Stevenson	Oxford
Treasure Island		Grosset & Dunlap
From These Comes Music	Hope Stoddard	Crowell
Pray Love, Remember	Mary Stolz	Harper
The Beatinest Boy	Jesse Stuart	Whittlesey House
A Penny's Worth of Character		Whittlesey House
North Star Shining	Hildegard Hoyt Swift	Morrow
Gulliver's Travels	Jonathan Swift	Grosset & Dunlap
The Book of Books	William Sypherd	Knopf
All-of-a-Kind Family	Sidney Taylor	Follett
More All-of-a-Kind Family		Follett
I Go A-Traveling	James S. Tippett	Harper
I Live in the City		Harper
I Know Some Little Animals		Harper
Silver Pennies	Blanche Thompson	Macmillan
Li Lun, Lad of Courage	Caroline Treffinger	Abingdon
The First Christmas	Robbie Trent	Harper
Rain Drop Splash	Alvin Tresselt	Lothrop, Lee & Shepard
White Snow, Bright Snow		Lothrop, Lee & Shepard
Follow the Wind		Lothrop, Lee & Shepard
Wake Up, Farm		Lothrop, Lee & Shepard
Pumpkin Moonshine	Tasha Tudor	Oxford
Snow for Christmas		Oxford
Adventures of Tom Sawyer	Mark Twain	Grosset & Dunlap
Adventures of Huckleberry Finn		Grosset & Dunlap
Magic Circle	Louis Untermeyer	Knopf
Rainbow in the Sky		Knopf

Stars to Steer By		Knopf
This Singing World		Knopf
Elizabeth Tudor: Sovereign Lady	Marguerite Vance	Dutton
The Jacksons of Tennessee		Dutton
On Wings of Fire (Rose Hawthorne)		Dutton
The Boy on the Road		Dutton
20,000 Leagues under the Sea	Jules Verne	Grosset & Dunlap
Whose Birthday Is It?	Nancy Watson	Knopf
The Animals Came First	Jean Welch	Oxford
Millet Tilled the Soil	Wheeler and Deucher	Dutton
Giotto Tended the Sheep		Dutton
Little House in the Big Woods	Laura Ingalls Wilder	Harper
Lillian Wald	Beryl Williams	Messner
Herbert	Hazel Wilson	Knopf
Herbert Again		Knopf
More Fun with Herbert		Knopf
Swiss Family Robinson	J. R. Wyss	Dutton
Amos Fortune	Elizabeth Yates	Farrar & Straus
Mountain Born		Coward
A Place for Peter		Coward
Once in the Year		Coward

In the classics listed above, often only one or two editions are given, although they are published in many editions. Grosset & Dunlap's *Illustrated Junior Library* is a very satisfying, inexpensive edition. Dodd, Mead; Dutton; Lippincott; Macmillan; Scribner; Winston; and World all publish excellent editions of classics. Many have beautiful illustrations.

8

Reading in Terms of Life

Will, then, the child of today and of the future read?

'Of all the arts of communication, the book is the one that goes straight for the individual. It is not tailored to a group audience, the product of many minds and speaking to many minds. It is the single individual speaking to the individual. . . . Since a book is durable almost to the point of immortality, it is able to wait until the individual is ready for it. . . . What is it that is waiting? It is the memory of man itself, the vast treasure of human knowledge and human delight that has been entrusted to paper since the invention of the written word. . . . It is as young as a leaf and as old as the oldest tree and next to fire, it is perhaps the luckiest thing that man ever stumbled upon.[1]

[1] Marchette Chute, from "Why Read Books?" *Scholastic Teacher*, Nov. 3, 1955.

A book can be a time-machine, turning back the years
To a violet-girl in bombazine,
A surly knavish Byzantine,
A buccaneering brigantine,
A monarch in arrears.

A book can be a cry through a sky that's moonsick,
A bead-eyed bat in a shadowy place,
The whistling sigh of a sound-quick broomstick
In space;

A wind-swung lantern at a pitch-black crossroads,
A snowball rolling toward obesity,
The secret blossom of a rock-hid moss-rose,
Twin old maids at the manse for tea.

A book can be a diamond (facets without end),
A baking-powder biscuit, a bow to bend,
A white-town dreaming in a hill's high pocket,
An eagle screaming over legions to the wars,
The jet-sped arch of a wild sky-rocket—
Burst into stars!

Down in alder-shadow by a chattering brook
A boy has just opened a new-found book.[2]

If these quotations describe books, if this is what reading can do for a child, surely we want our children to read. Reading can be a resource for developing such qualities of character as justness, reverence for personality, respect for human dignity, kindness, and generosity. Since such qualities are the basis of a good life in a free, democratic society, then surely that society should make sure that children have books and want to read them. If anyone thinks of reading as merely word recognition —whether through sounding out the word or recognizing it by form or letter grouping—such a person may not be concerned with human use of that skill. Most people use a skill only if it brings them some satisfaction. Reading is far more than a simple ability; it involves many skills. It is a highly complex

[2] Carl Carmer, *What a Book Can Be.* Published in *New York Herald Tribune,* 1955.

experience involving learning as it is continuous with living—living which involves thinking and making decisions, for one-self or as part of a group, and acting accordingly. Thomas Merton once said this very simply:

> To inform a mind is to impart a new form to it; that is to give it a new and more cogent reality. A mind that reads will enter into a deep and vital activity; it begins to live a more nearly perfect and satisfying way. A man who really reads gains by his reading a fuller existence. He acquires a new spiritual stature, a new peace.

Children should begin by reading the books which are close to their specific needs and interests, not those imposed by a parent or teacher or those on a list which must be read because these selected books can do certain things for the reader. Some children rebel vigorously against what they call "ought" books. Compelling certain kinds of reading regardless of whether or not the child is ready for it may easily kill the most eager interest in books.

This conversation was overheard in a sixth grade classroom:

"I never choose one of those 'ought' books."

"Doncha?"

"Naw. They're too slow, too long."

"Ever read *Little House in the Big Woods?* It's swell."

"Naw. I read Tom Sawyer and Huck Finn. She says they're 'ought' books, but they're good. Gee, I still run around with Huck in my mind."

"Try *Treasure Island,* too. You'll like it."

"Do things happen? I like to read, but things gotta happen and fast."

To mean anything to its reader, the book must meet him where he *is* in his development, his thinking, and his feeling, not where some adult thinks he ought to be! And once loved, a book may remain important to a child for years. Nancy wrote home from college right after Thanksgiving of her freshman year, "I forgot my copy of *The Christ Child.* How can I get ready for Christmas without it?"

Frank G. Jennings says it thus:[3]

Reading is at the very least a two way process between what someone writes and what someone understands and the frightening difference between the two. It also involves what happens because of this understanding. The literary experience is one of the most profound mind-shaping events in the life of man. It kept cultures alive through the campfire story-teller. It makes it possible for Plato and Christ to instruct us from thousands of years away. It joins minds and times together for the better management and control of our universe. It is as precise and practical as a door latch. It is the golden goad that makes man humane. It is this that we want our children to discover.

"Reading to meet my needs, my interests" may well be the child's first requirement. There are certain things a child may expect from reading a book; in fact, unless the book does these for him, he may be quite justified in not reading it.

First of all, it illumines experience: a little, if the experience brought to the book is scanty; much, if the experience brought is rich. It explains facts by description and clarification. It narrates adventure—past or present—so that we absorb the whole experience as we would one of our own. It shows us the life of a person so like ourselves—or what we would like to become—that we live and learn by true identification. It makes us feel and understand such beauty or ugliness, joy or sorrow, earthliness or spirituality, that our experience is illumined even as the sun brightens the day.

Secondly, the book should contribute to our growth, not only equipping us for the experience but encouraging and inspiring us to go on. The informative book of science such as *How Your Body Works, You and Your Amazing Mind;* the challenging book about some strong interest or desire such as *Discovering Design, From These Comes Music;* the exciting biography like *Albert Schweitzer, Twelve Citizens of the World:* all should be the right book at the right time to contribute to growth.

Also, the living book places all experience in its place in the total picture of the universe. It gives a sense of relationship—

[3] Frank Jennings, in *The Saturday Review*, Feb. 4, 1956.

relativity—the understanding of which makes easier personal fulfillment and adjustment to a good way of life.

A book is an affair of the heart as well as of the mind. A good book has a good plot, moving action. Even the troubadour singing his news knew the value of that in holding his audience. The folk tales that live through the centuries create and solve a problem, but so does a comic strip or pulp story. Necessary as a good plot line is, the book that *lives* must go farther to create characters and atmosphere. There must be a universality underlying the specific characteristics of the individual character. Universal human need, human awareness, or human response can take books beyond ephemeral interest. Such a book is close to the heart and mind of all men, not just a man here or there, now or then. This is not to say that the action or character is not delineated in terms of a specific action or place; that treatment makes him vivid, living. But the same situation could have occurred in terms of its basic relations in many places or times.

The child says, "This could have been me." The psychological identification is so complete that the reader feels the book cannot end; he cannot stop living the experience he is reading. He, himself, is an integral part of it. As the moment of reading stops, the reader goes on living and creates what happens next and next and next. As the sixth grader said, "I still run around with Huck Finn in my mind." There must be something beyond the joy or satisfaction of sharing the experience in the book. A kind of residue enters into the reader and becomes a part of his continuing self: a psychological reality, a spiritual value, a sum of overtones and undertones. This quality can be called by many names: reality, beauty, humor, integrity, or perhaps all of these. Reading a book which becomes a part of one's being is a creative act involving both author and reader. It is this action which makes it part of life itself. Then, too, a book is an art form, and as such, is not merely the self-expression of one individual. The very fact that it is read makes it part of the evolving form our common life is taking.

Perhaps it is well here to think about what makes a book good enough to read and reread, good enough to live with. Joan asked, "What makes you say these mysteries are trash and *Little House in the Big Woods* is so wonderful? How do you know?" Her friend asked her if her mother had a diamond ring. "Of course. My father gave it to her."

"Have you one?"

"Not yet, but I have a pretty 10¢ store ring."

"Does it have a diamond?"

"Of course not."

"How do you know?"

Soon she was explaining how she knew. "I get it!" she exclaimed. "How does one know?" There are some criteria with which we may begin.

First, one should consider the purpose of a book. It may be:

to inform
to explain
to develop desirable attitudes and values
to contribute to understanding ourselves, others, our environment, and the past
to give insight
to increase awareness
to entertain
to stimulate imagination
to inspire

A real writer has something to say. He writes from an inner compulsion, transmitting his living and thinking into words that others may read. A book may meet one or several of these purposes. If its main purpose is to develop certain attitudes or values, one must beware of propagandizing or being biased. Readers grow to trust the author who is able to communicate his thoughts successfully and fulfill the purpose or purposes of his book.

The content of the book may be anything in the world that interests a potential reader. If factual, the material should be accurate, up-to-date, carefully organized. The book is likely to be more useful if it has a good table of contents and is carefully indexed. The presentation of facts should be objective. Biography and historic fiction should be authentic, and warm and human in presentation. Stories should have a good plot, convincing characterization, realistic background, and a mood that fits the nature of the tale. Most children today like plenty of action. A swift-paced story is much more likely to be read than a slow one. We live in a fast moving world.

Such values as honesty, fair play, and accepted social patterns ought to characterize the content. The material should be within the interest span and comprehension of the reader. This does not mean writing down to a child; it may mean writing up, with high selectivity that demands great skill. It does not mean that one writes for a second grader with a so-called second-grade vocabulary. The aural and recognition vocabulary of even a seven-year-old is in the thousands. Interest is much more likely to determine the recognizable vocabulary than any other motivation. The content may be anything of interest to potential readers from stones to stars, from true historical events to the wildest creations of the imagination, but the book must be readable. The way this content is presented is called the style of the writing. Overlong, involved sentences make people call this author's style uninteresting, heavy, stodgy. The way of writing should be appropriate to the subject matter and purpose of the book. In all factual, informative books, a simple, clear, concise style is appropriate. In fiction, whatever carries on the action of the story, makes the characters live and creates the mood for the reader to share is the appropriate style for that book. As music has to do with the order of notes and tempo, so writing is concerned with the order and selection of words and phrases and total movement—whether slow as in *lento* or quick as in *allegro*. The writing within one book should be consistent in sentence and paragraph structure, whether the writing is smooth or flowing, rhythmic, incisive, or staccato. It must be clear enough to hold the reader's interest and original and interesting enough to communicate with the reader in the author's unique way. If many people discover that a author has something worthwhile to say to them and says it well, it is probable that he has a good style of writing.

If one is to go a step farther and judge the literary worth of a book, other standards are involved: universality of appeal of the characters, the lasting worth and interest of the subject matter, the concern with basic values such as beauty, humor, integrity, spiritual awareness. The quality of the writing style, which must communicate with a large number of readers, is also a factor in judging the literary worth of a book. If illustrated, the illustrations should be appropriate to the subject matter and have appeal for the child. Factual material needs accurate charts, graphs, or photographs. Imaginative illustrations may use widely varied techniques in color and design. A wide variety of artistic worth provides a wide variety of appeal. It is well to remember that taste develops slowly, and that not all people—even the critics—evaluate good art in the same way. It is interesting to note that these are criteria we would establish for any book—for an adult reader as well as for a child.

Format is important in all books, but certain aspects are particularly important in children's. A readable type should be carefully selected. Length of line and spacing are important in making the page easy to read. The paper should be suited to the use of the book and also contribute to the ease of reading. The consensus seems to be that reading type on glazed paper is not as easy as reading a dull-finished page. Also, an off-white seems to be easier on the eyes than a pure white. Good binding insures durability. Harmony between the book's appearance and its content is likely to add to its appeal. Some books, produced with great care and consideration, achieve distinguished and beautiful appearance. There are many such today, even in this age of mass production.

The authors and artists are citizens of the child's world as well as of the adult world. Sometimes people say that the true artist never grows up in spite of having a mature mind; this is no contradiction. The heart of a child is necessary for a citizen of the kingdom of heaven and the kingdom of earth. Creative people are good companions for children. Faithful to the essence of art, they make beauty characteristic of their work. They make it possible for the reader to share universal experience. They respect the individual. They appreciate the release that joy, humor, and tears can bring to a human being. They are aware of the value of knowledge—of the heart as well as of the mind. Their freedom in the use of words, in the use of color, line, and design, encourages a child's exercise of freedom. Their integrity leads to a basic morality, not just the morals or mores of a given time, but a universal, deep morality of the human mind and spirit. Books written by such creative writers and artists continue to live as an integral part of the life of children growing up in a democratic society.

Margaret Wise Brown, Virginia Lee Burton, Edgar and Ingri d'Aulaire, Francoise, Wanda Gag, Zhenya Gay, Dorothy Lathrop, Robert McCloskey, Leo Politi, Beatrix Potter, the Haders, the Petershams, Miriam Schlein, Tasha Tudor, and Leonard Weisgard are a few of the special author-artist friends of young children and all lovers of beauty. Valenti Angelo, Laura Armer, Caroline Sherwin Bailey, Mary and Conrad Buff, Ann Nolan Clark, Catherine Coblentz, Olivia Coolidge, Alice Dalgliesh, James Daugherty, Marguerite De Angeli, Meindert De Jong, Esther Forbes, Genevieve Foster, Doris Gates, Rumer Godden, Elizabeth Janet Gray, Marguerite Henry, Elizabeth Orton Jones, Eleanor Estes, Eleanor Lattimore, Robert Lawson, Marie Lawson, Meridel Le Seuer, Katherine Milhous, May McNeer, Ruth Sawyer, Kate Seredy, Garth Williams, Laura Ingalls Wilder are wonderful friends to children a little older and all who still hold wonder in their hearts. It is impossible to mention all the authors whose entrance through books into our children's lives assures reading a place in the American way of life.

Books, authors, artists, children: they belong together in all living that truly extends one's life space. Most children want to read; most children will read if books that meet their needs, their interests, and their living are easily available. *Reading is living*.

Reading is the creative act through which the mind and heart of mankind, transmitted through author and artist, enter the child's being and thus return to the life stream.

> Books are more than words,
> More than birds'
> Flight, more than song;
> They last long.[4]

[4] Joseph Joel Keith, from *Books*. Reprinted by permission of the author and *The Saturday Review*.